# Embrace Your Journey
## A Coloring Book for Navigating Life

by Roxanne Glaser

Embrace Your Journey: A Coloring Book for Navigating Life

ISBN 978-1-79420-332-7

Second Edition 2024
SDG Design Publications
Waco, Texas, 76712

Hi, friends!

Welcome to the Embrace Your Journey Coloring Book.

Inside are 50 pages for you to color and doodle on; all hand-illustrated for your enjoyment. Coloring and doodling calms your mind and relaxes your body allowing you to become present in the moment. It is the perfect antidote for our hectic, modern life with screens and notifications always pulling our attention.

I recommend using fine tipped markers, colored pencils, or gel pens. Check out www.superdoodlegirl.com for a list of my favorites. All of them can easily be found at any local craft store or online. Some of the doodle details can be difficult to capture with crayons, but you can certainly use them if you prefer. If you use markers, slip a sheet of paper between the pages to prevent bleed-through.

Remember, coloring should be relaxing. Focus on the movement of the pen or pencil and let go of any expectations of perfection. My artwork is whimsical, quirky, and definitely not perfect. My joy comes from making it. My intention is to provide you with an opportunity to become present in your day and encourage you in your journey, so enjoy!

Hugs + Doodles,

@SuperDoodleGirl

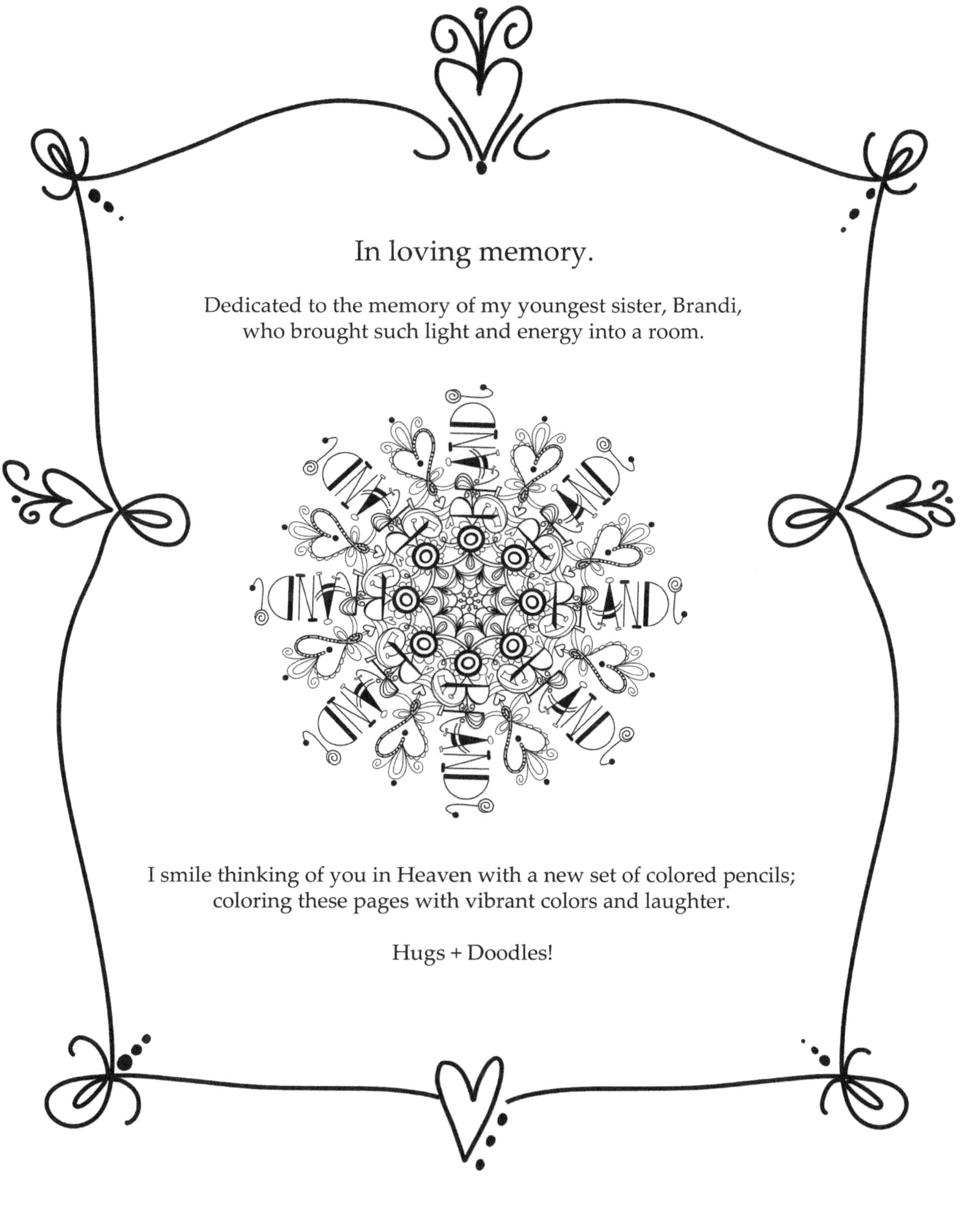

In loving memory.

Dedicated to the memory of my youngest sister, Brandi,
who brought such light and energy into a room.

I smile thinking of you in Heaven with a new set of colored pencils;
coloring these pages with vibrant colors and laughter.

Hugs + Doodles!

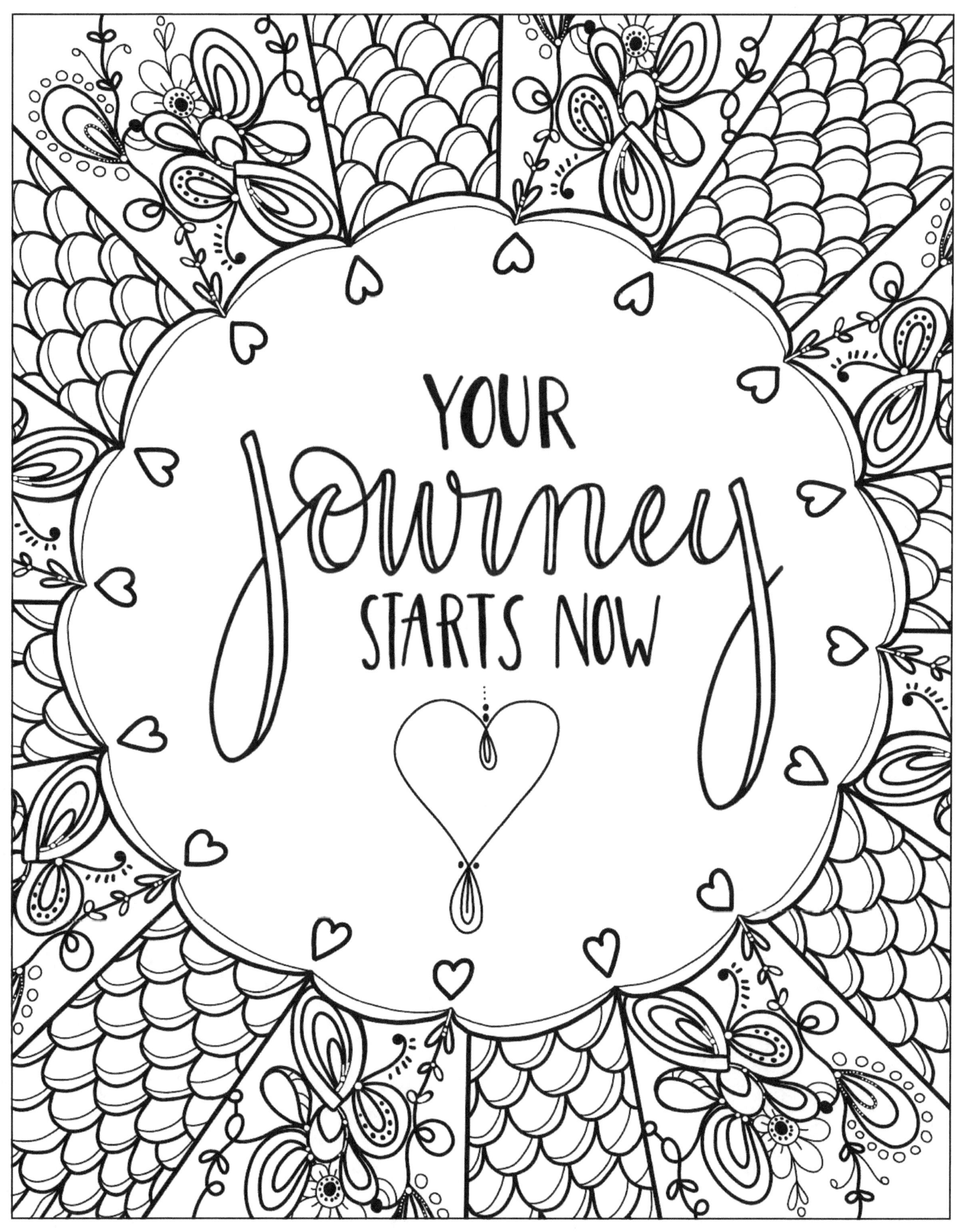

YOUR
Journey
STARTS NOW

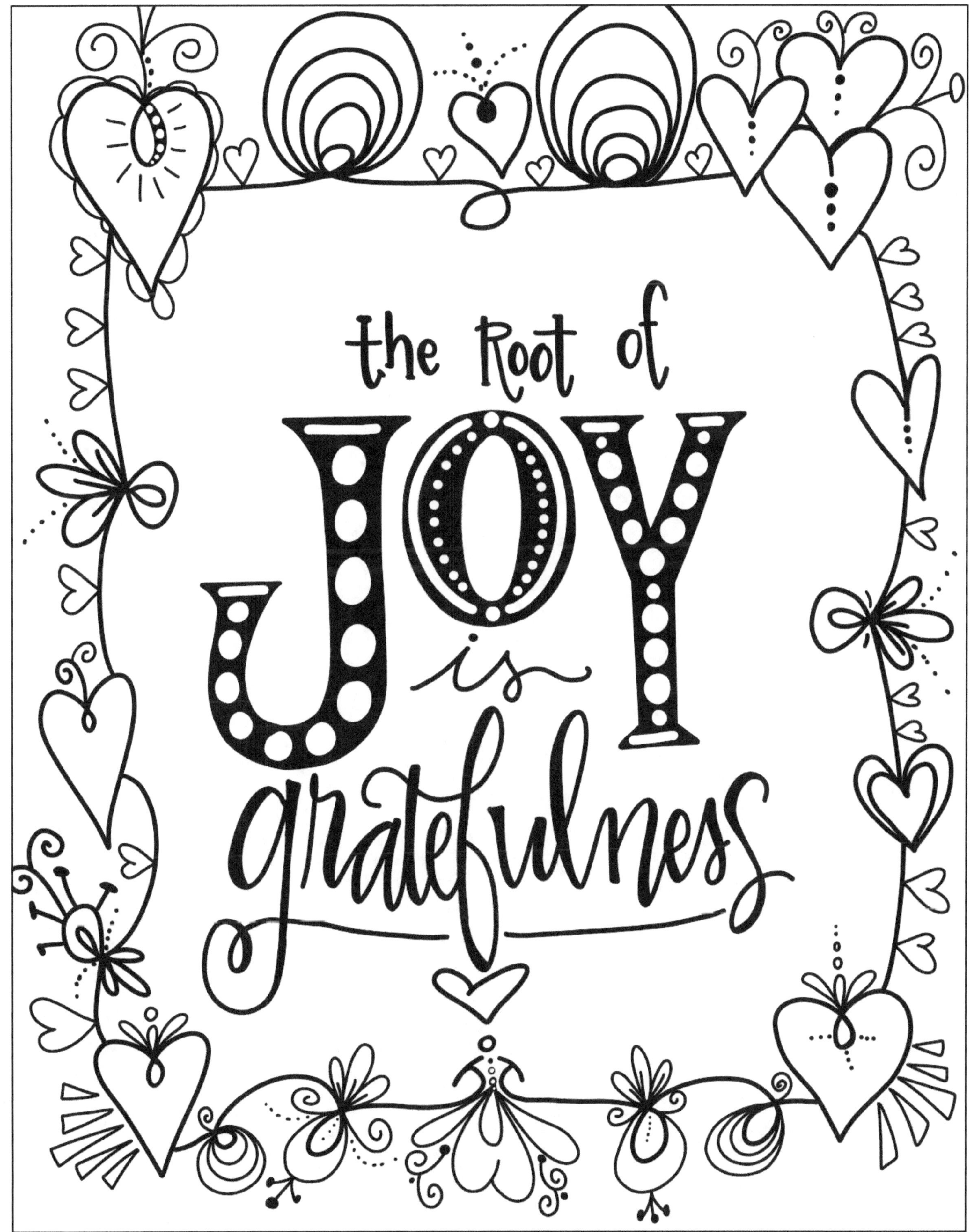

the Root of
JOY
is
gratefulness

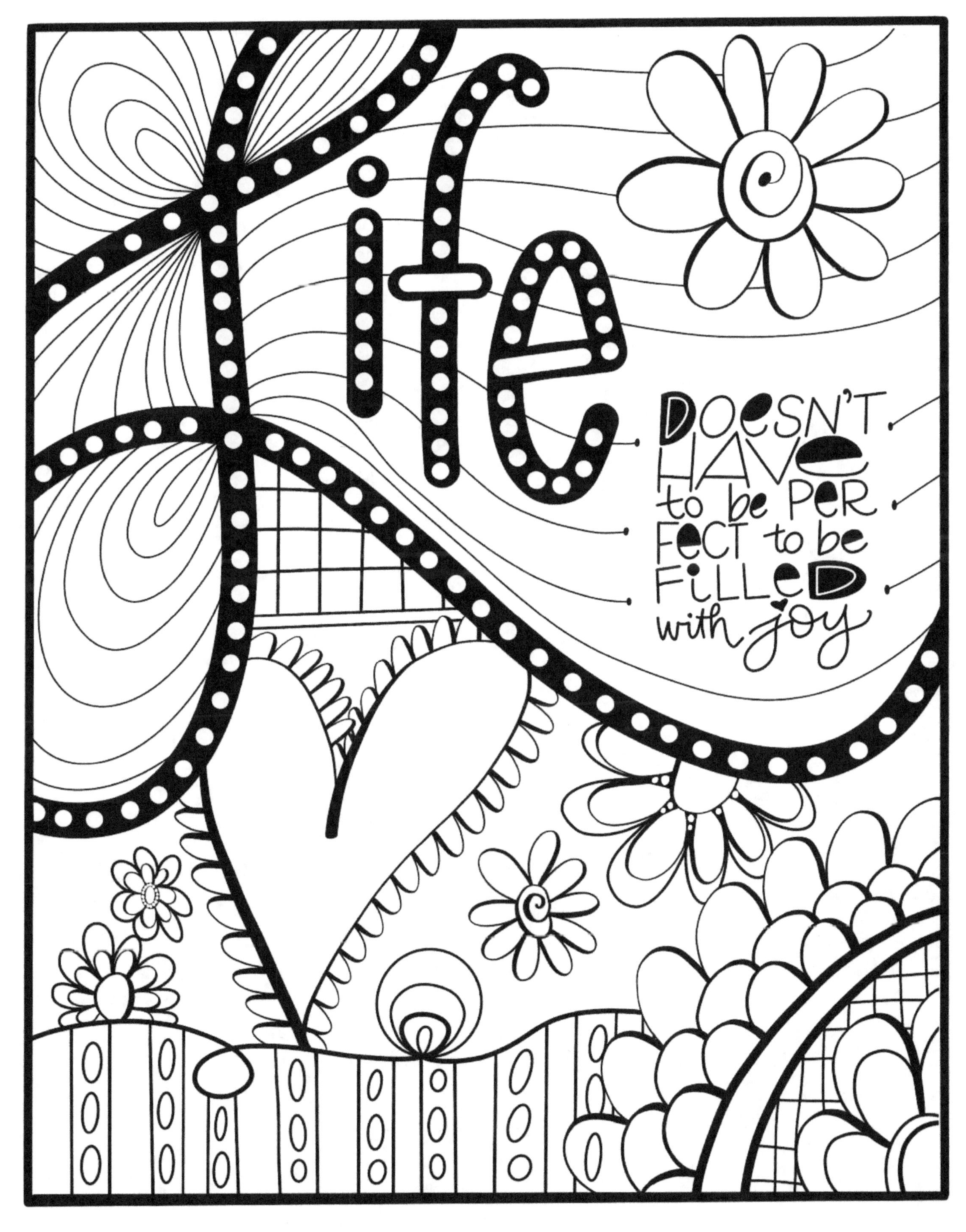

life
Doesn't Have to be PerFect to be FillED with joy

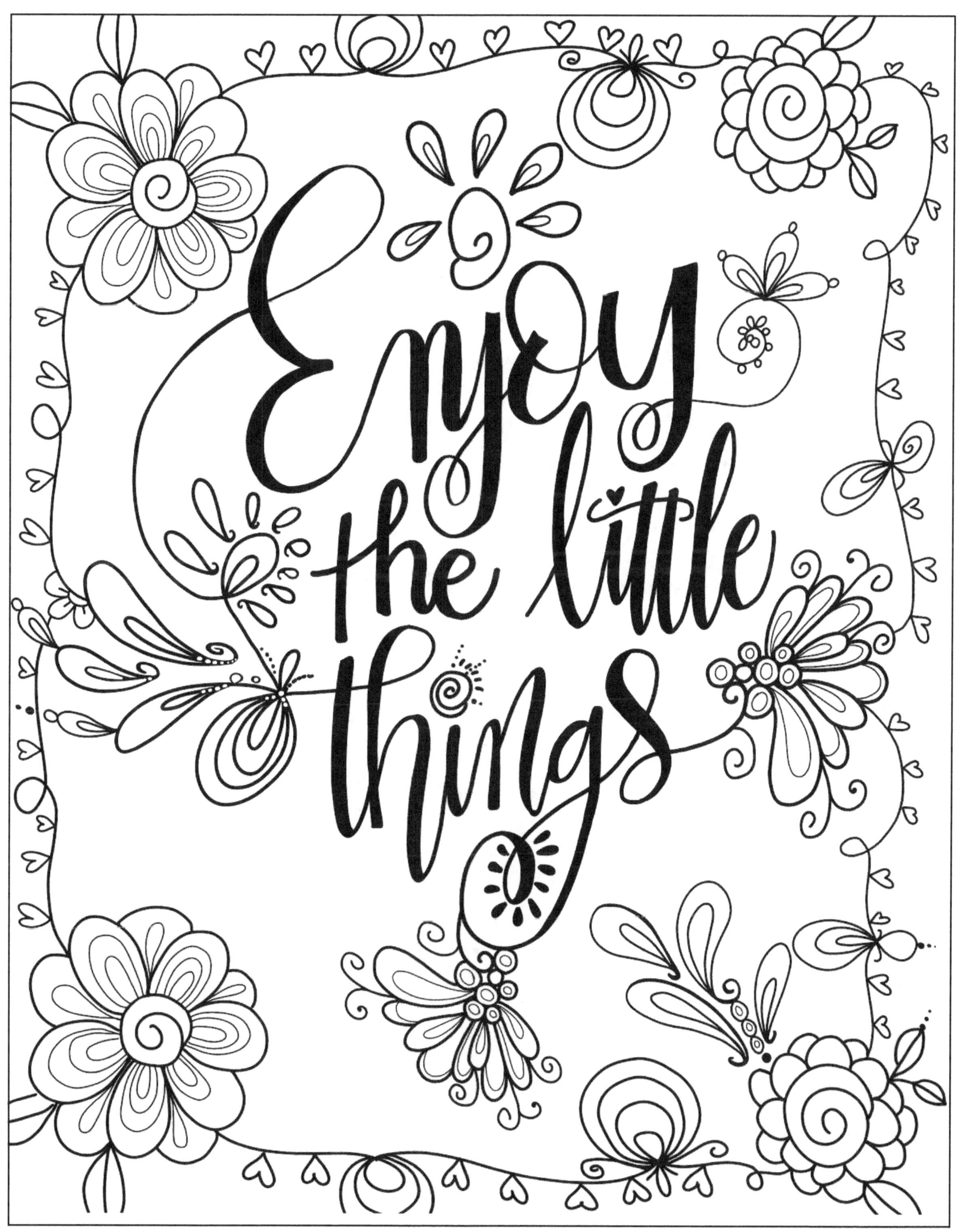

Enjoy the little things

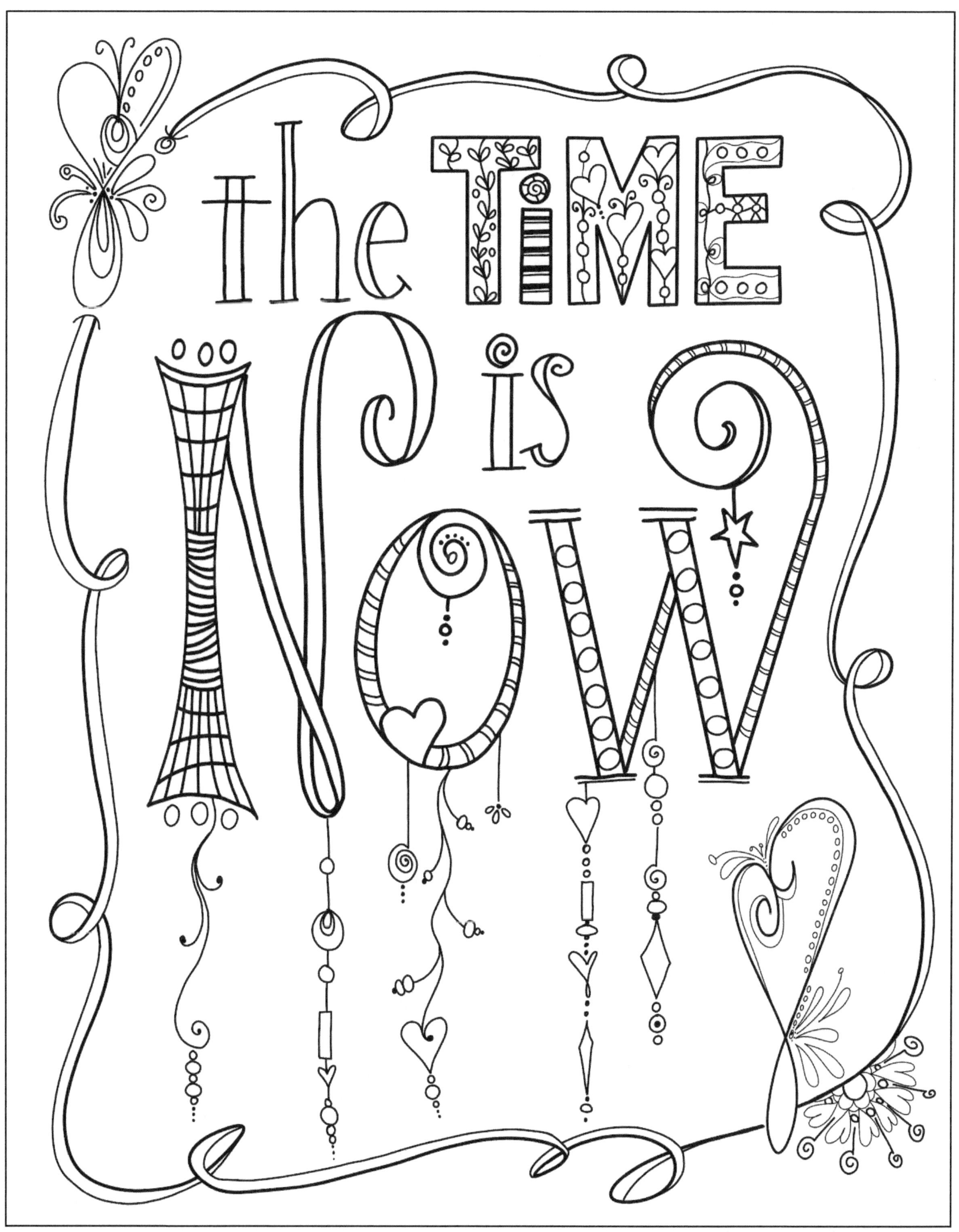

the TiME is NOW

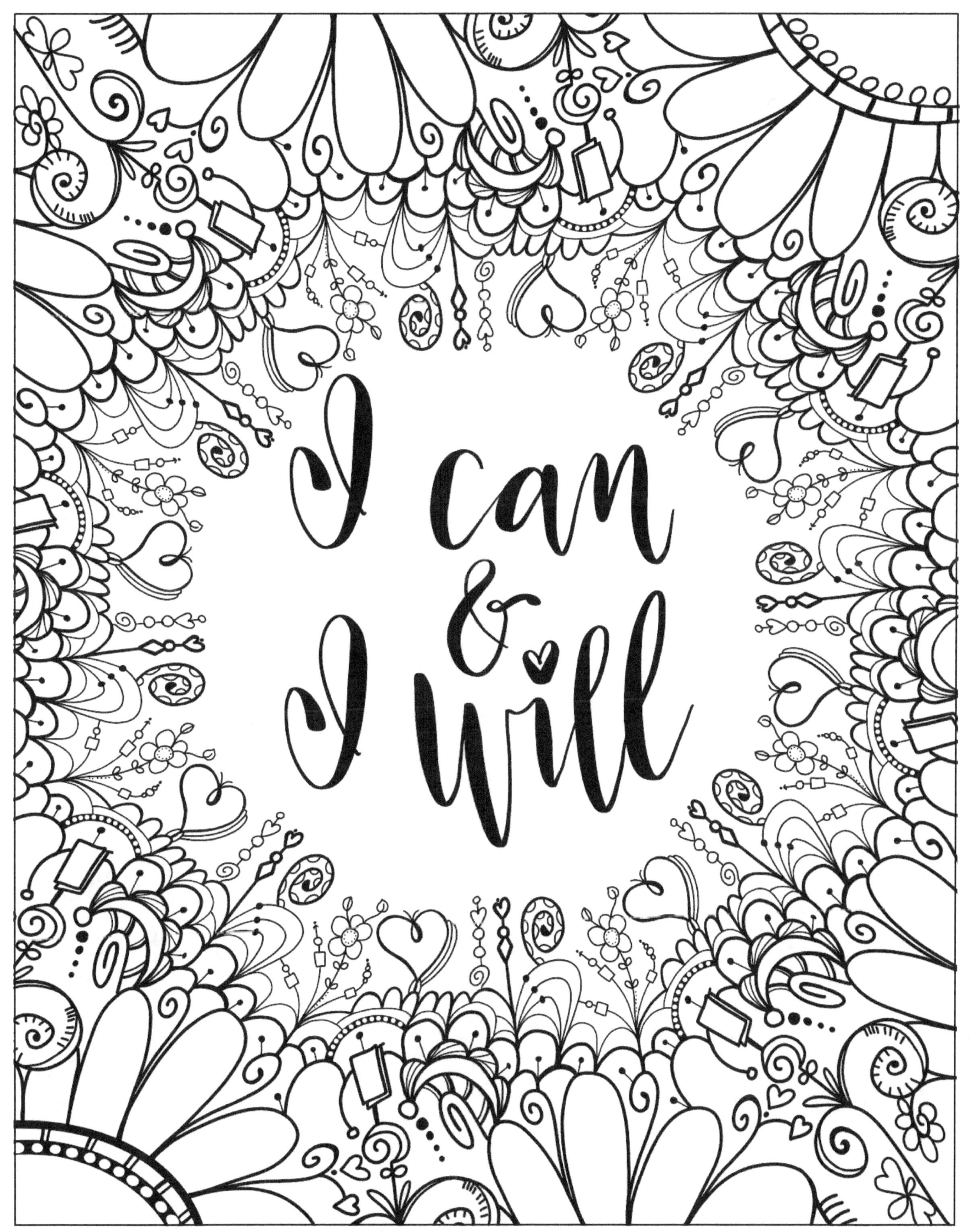
I can
&
I will

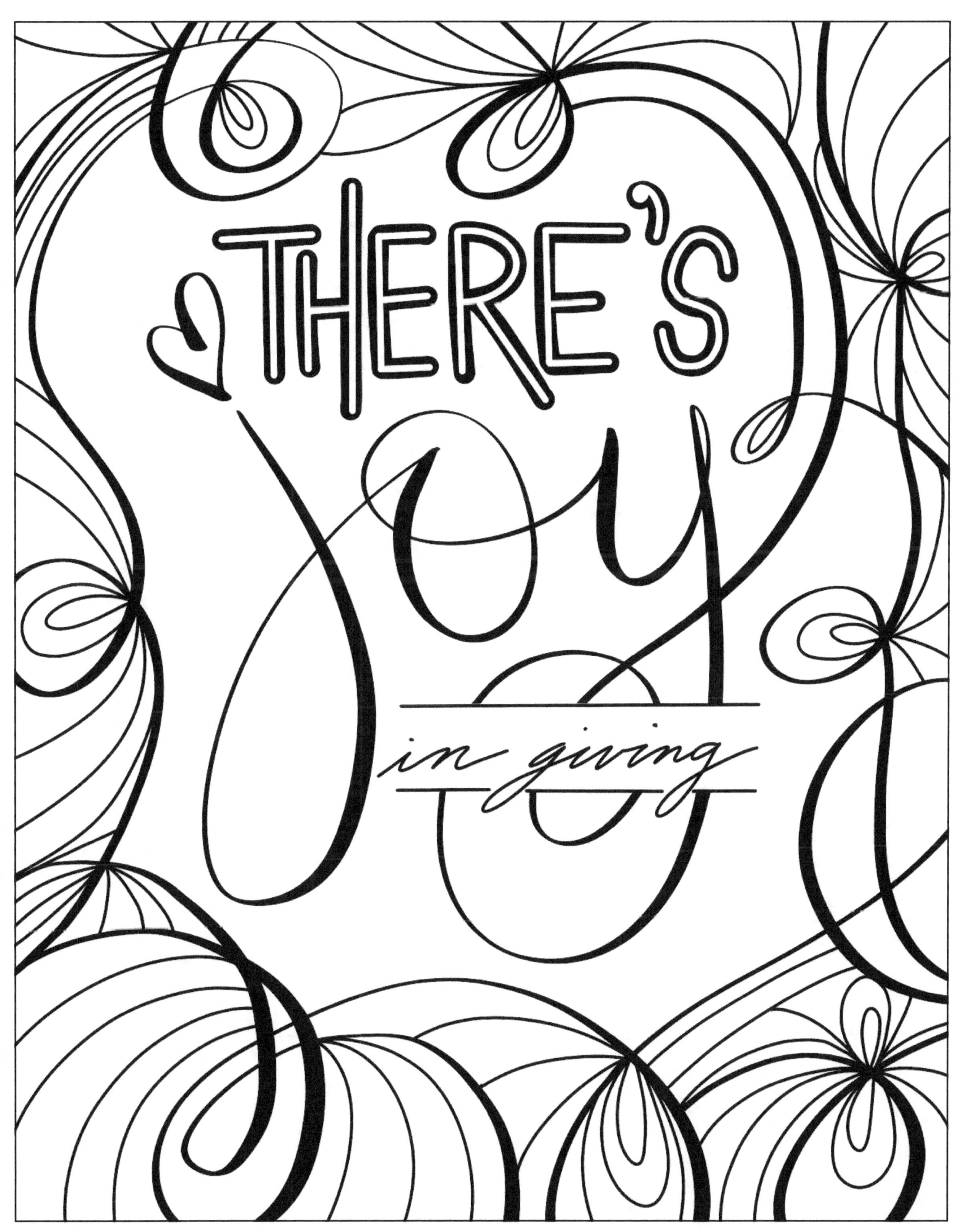

THERE'S
JOY
in giving

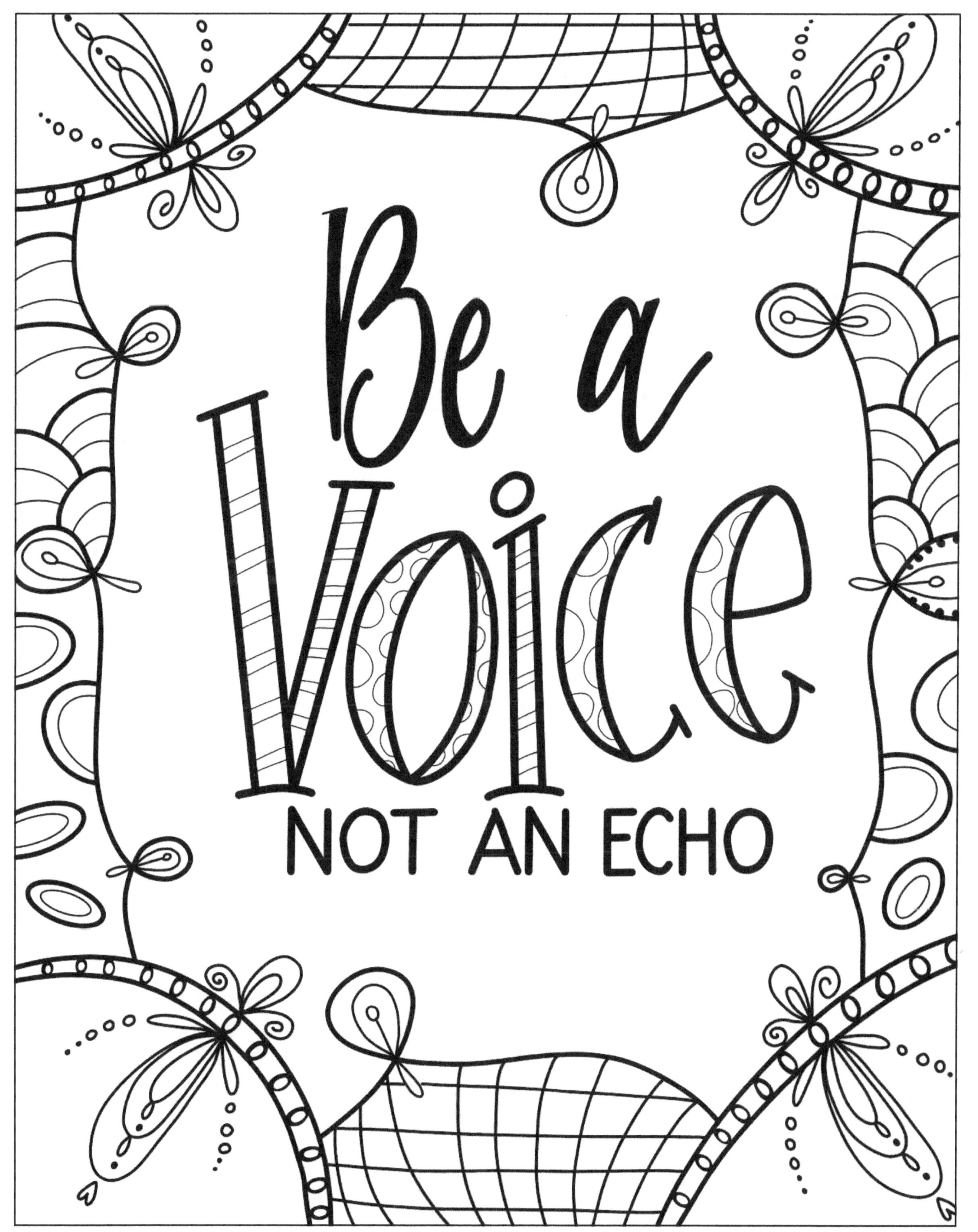

Be a
Voice
NOT AN ECHO

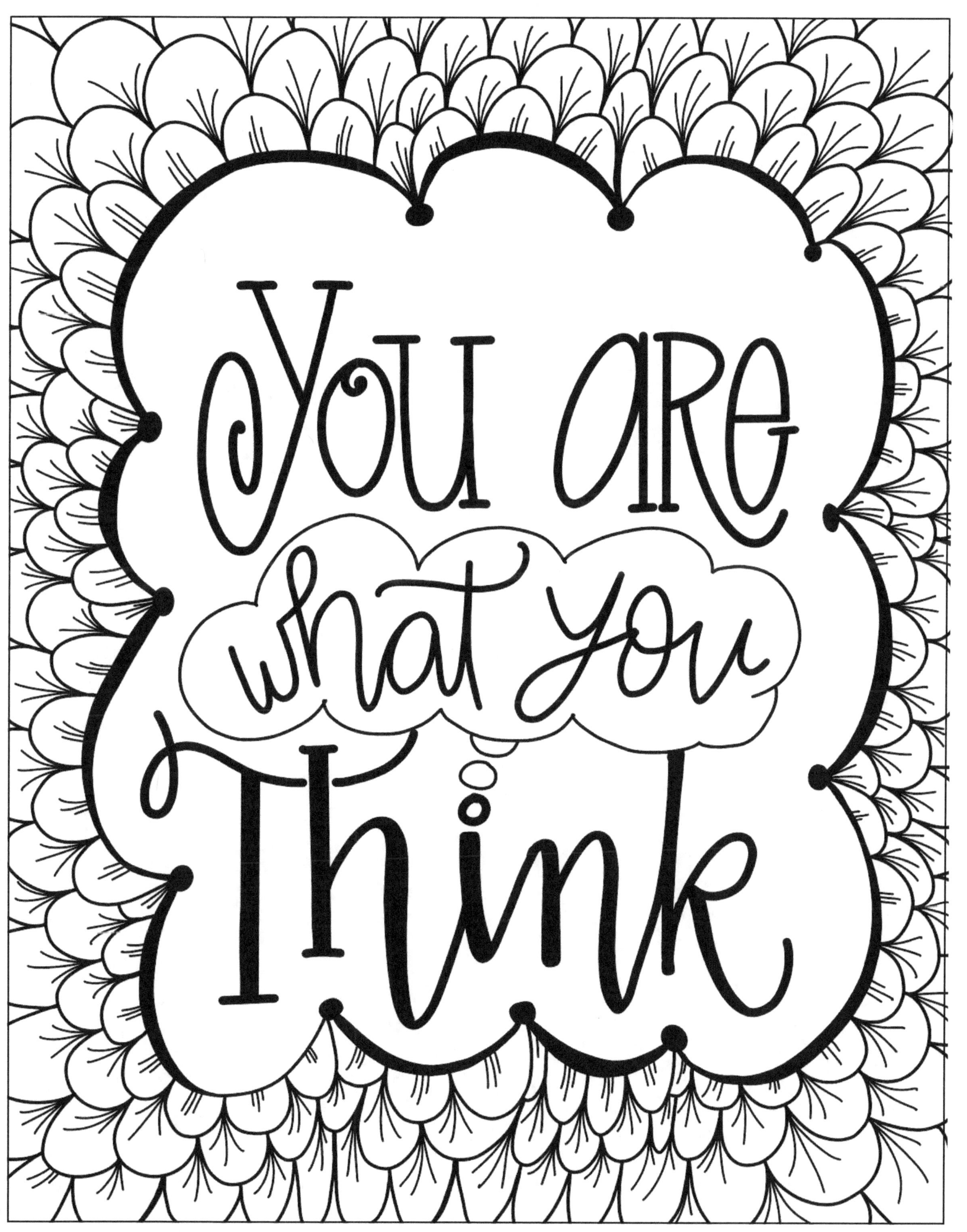
You are
what you
Think

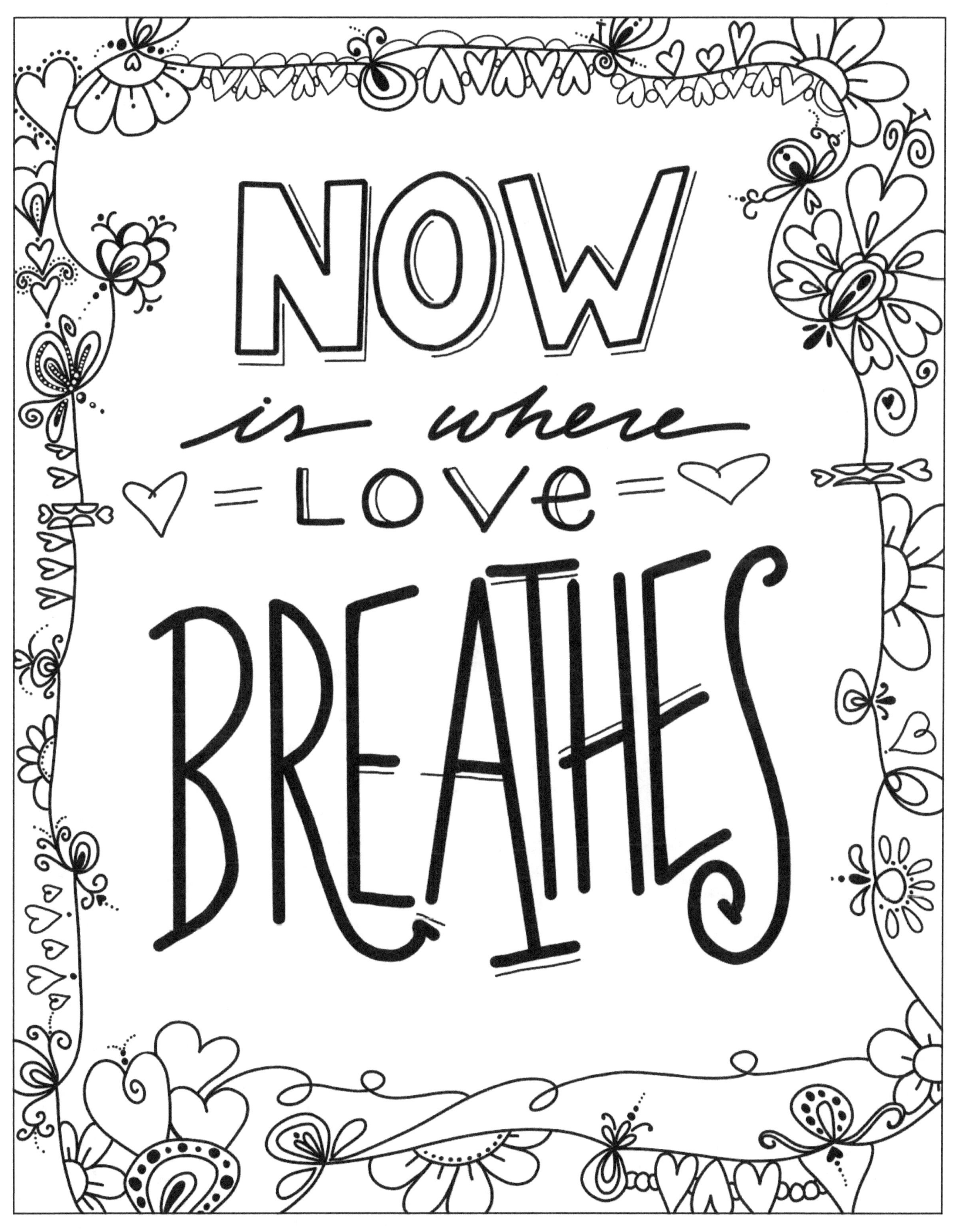

NOW
is where
LOVE
BREATHES

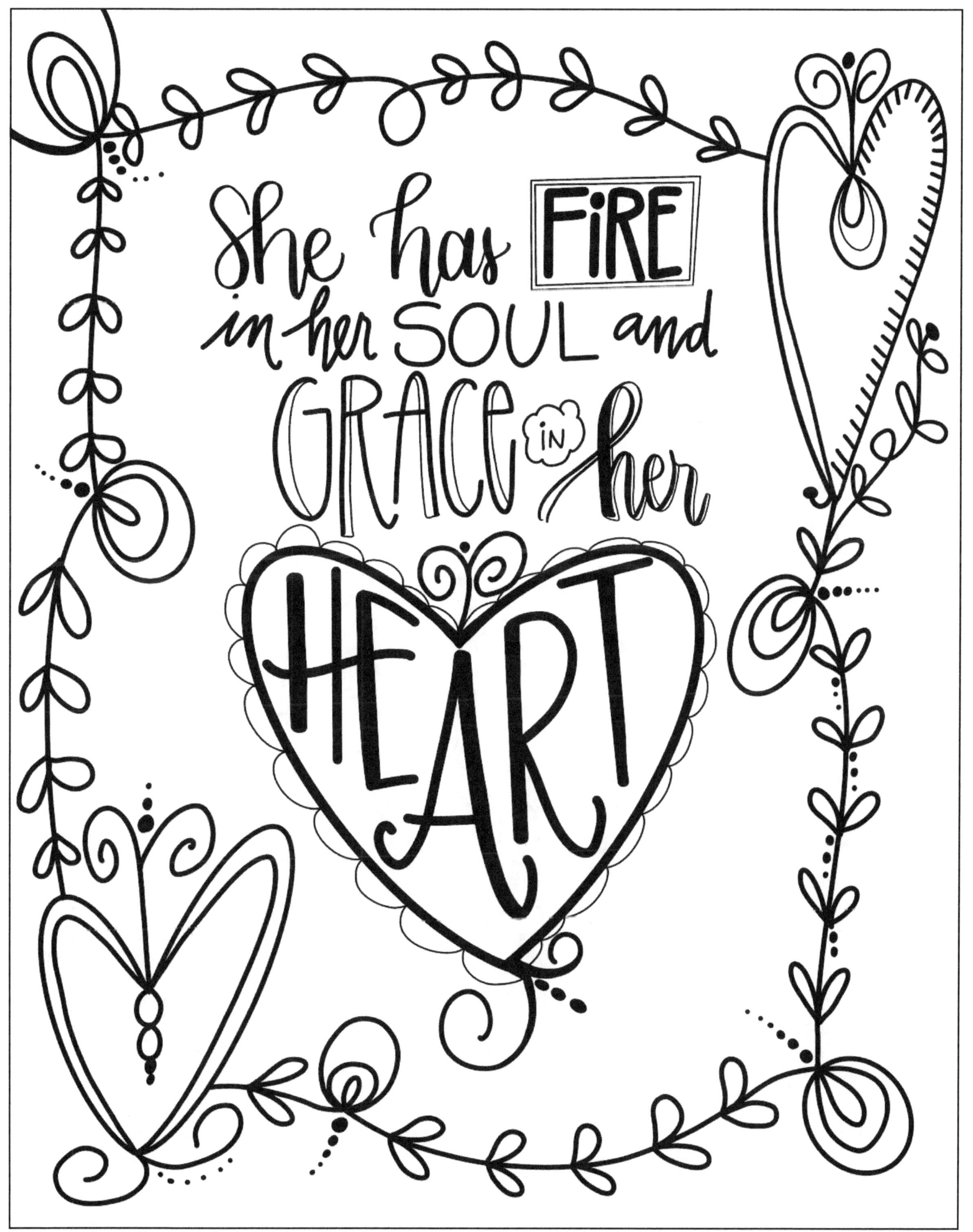

She has FIRE
in her SOUL and
GRACE in her
HEART

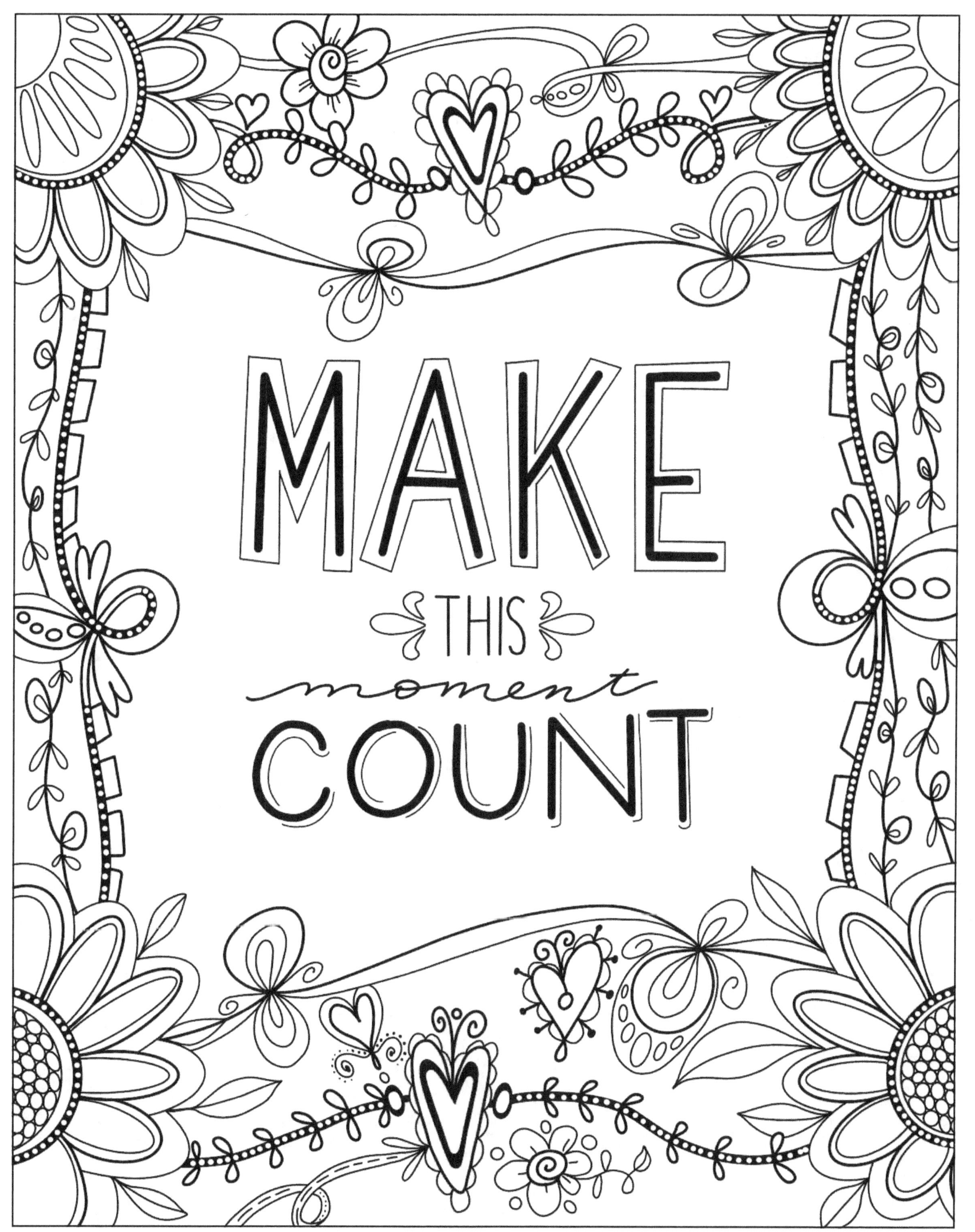

MAKE
THIS
moment
COUNT

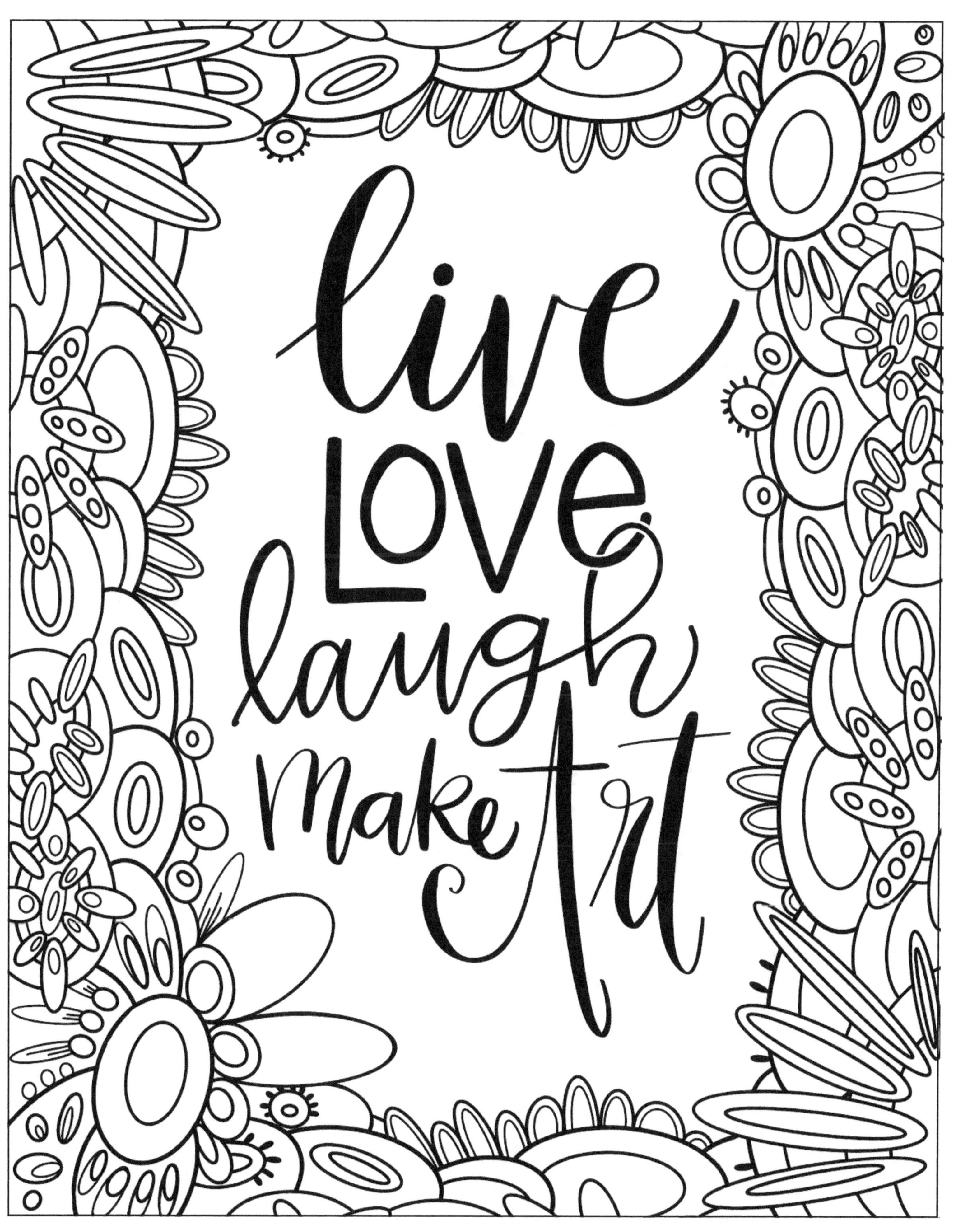

live
love
laugh
make Art

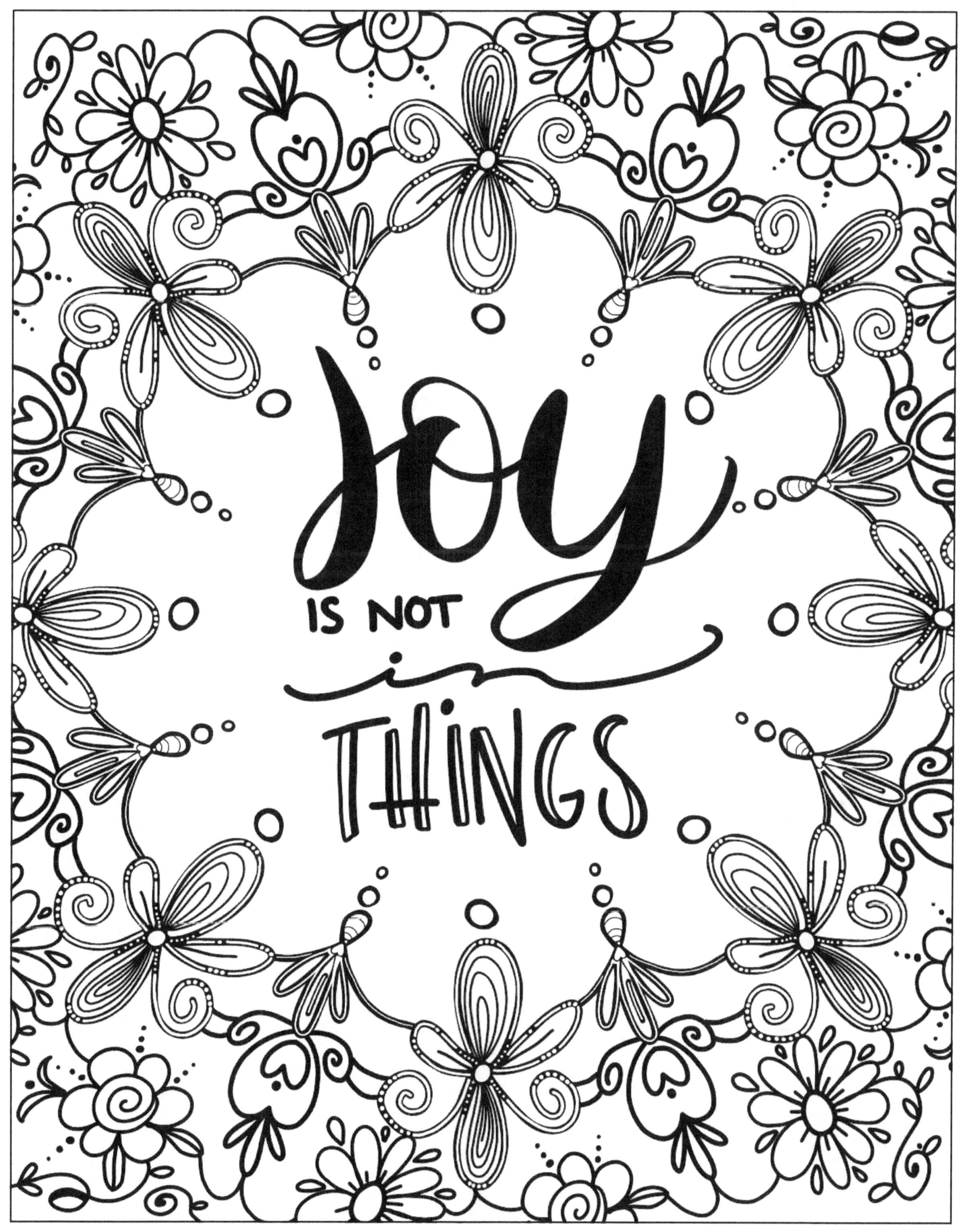

JOY
IS NOT
IN
THINGS

live your
DREAM
Share your
PASSION

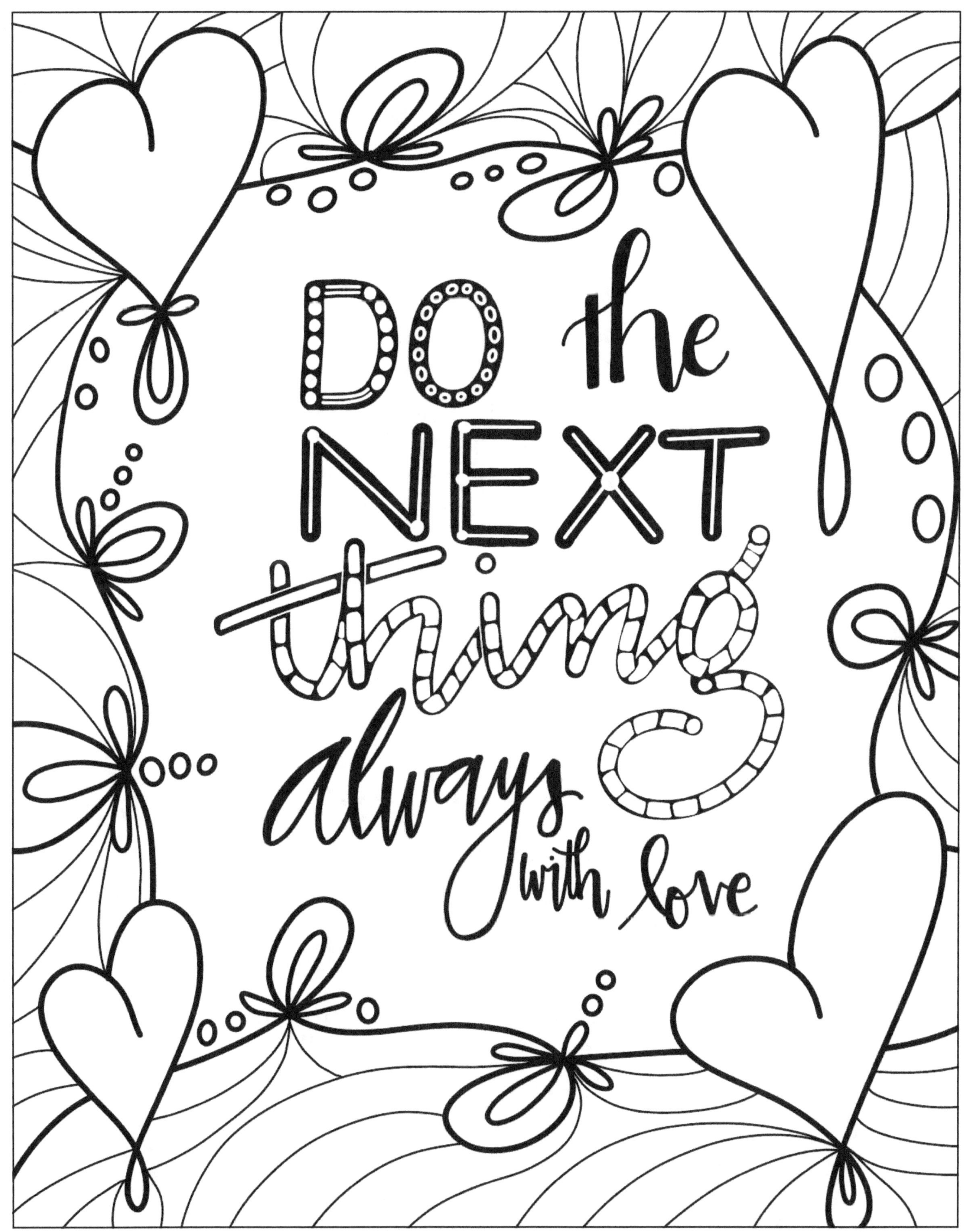
Do the
NEXT
thing
always
with love

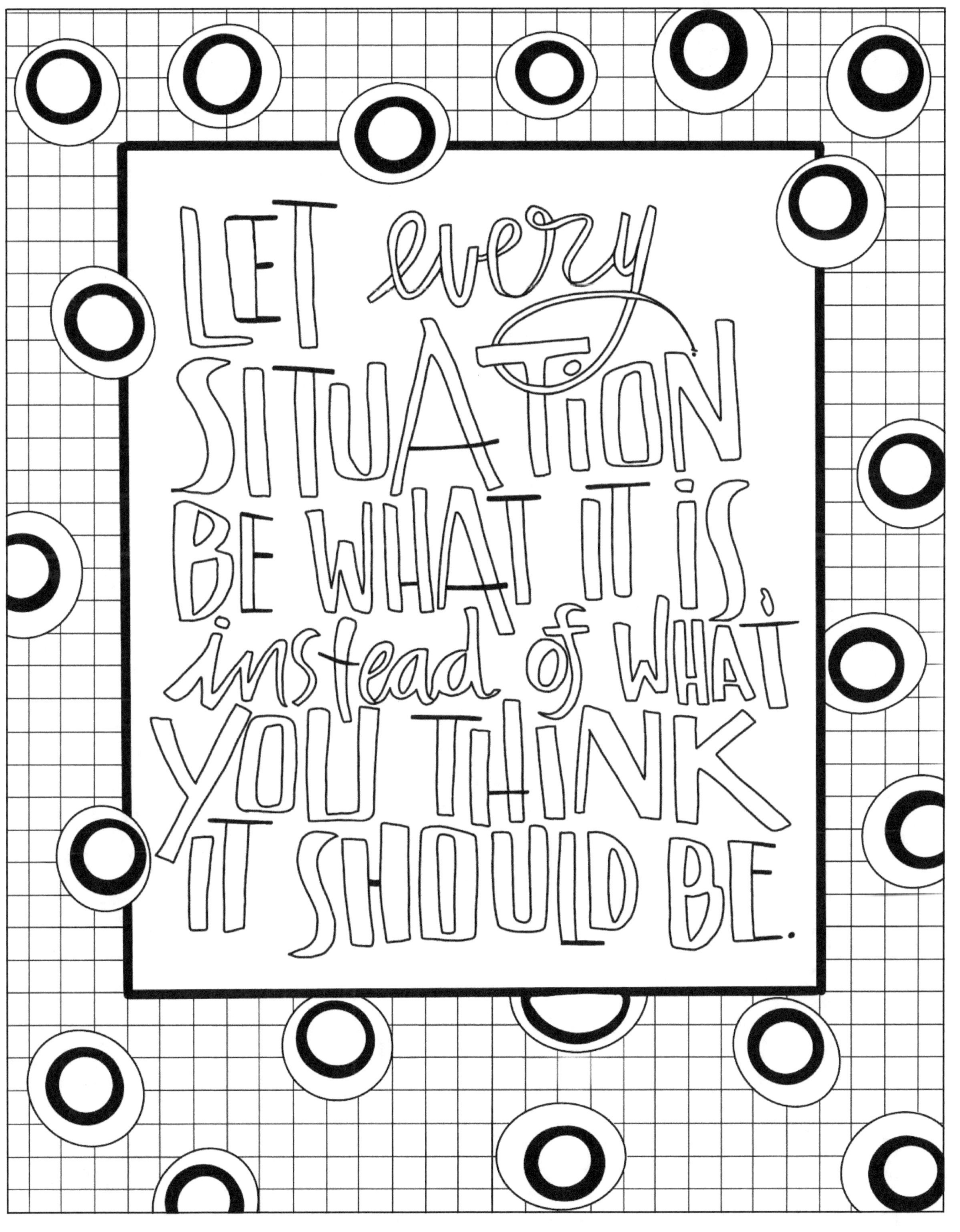

LET every SITUATION BE WHAT IT IS, instead of WHAT YOU THINK IT SHOULD BE.

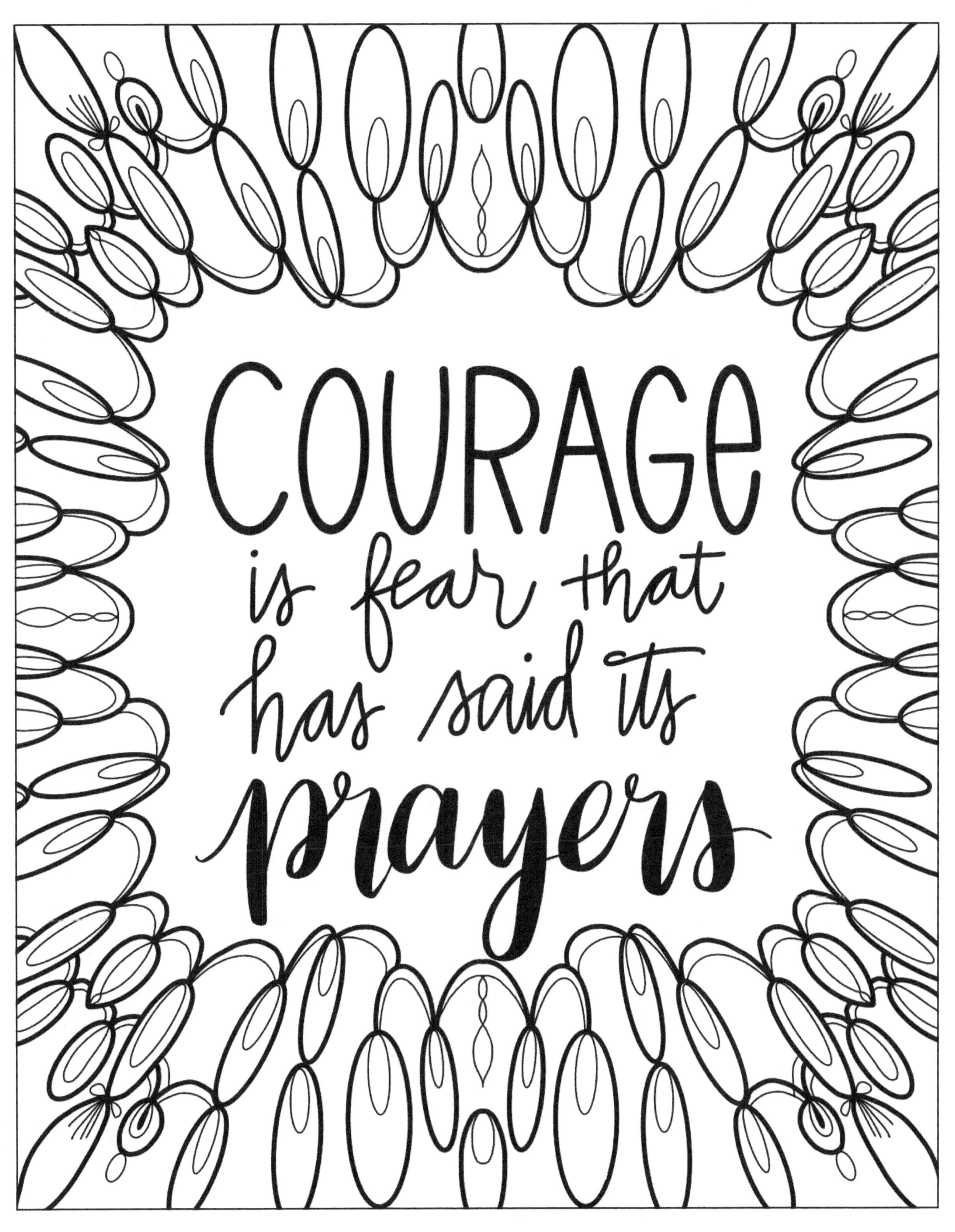

COURAGE
is fear that
has said its
prayers

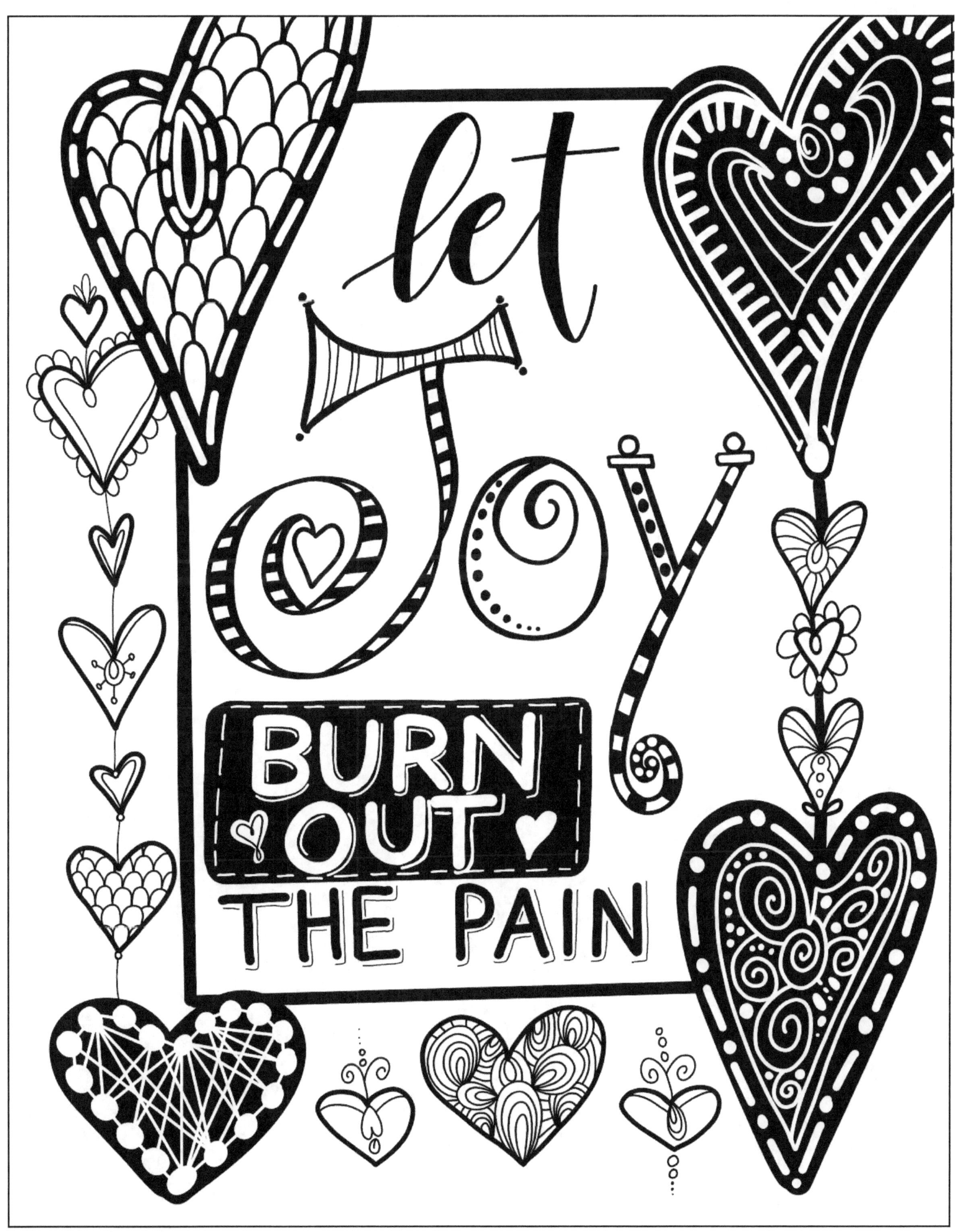

Let
Joy
BURN OUT
THE PAIN

make a
WISH
the universe
is listening

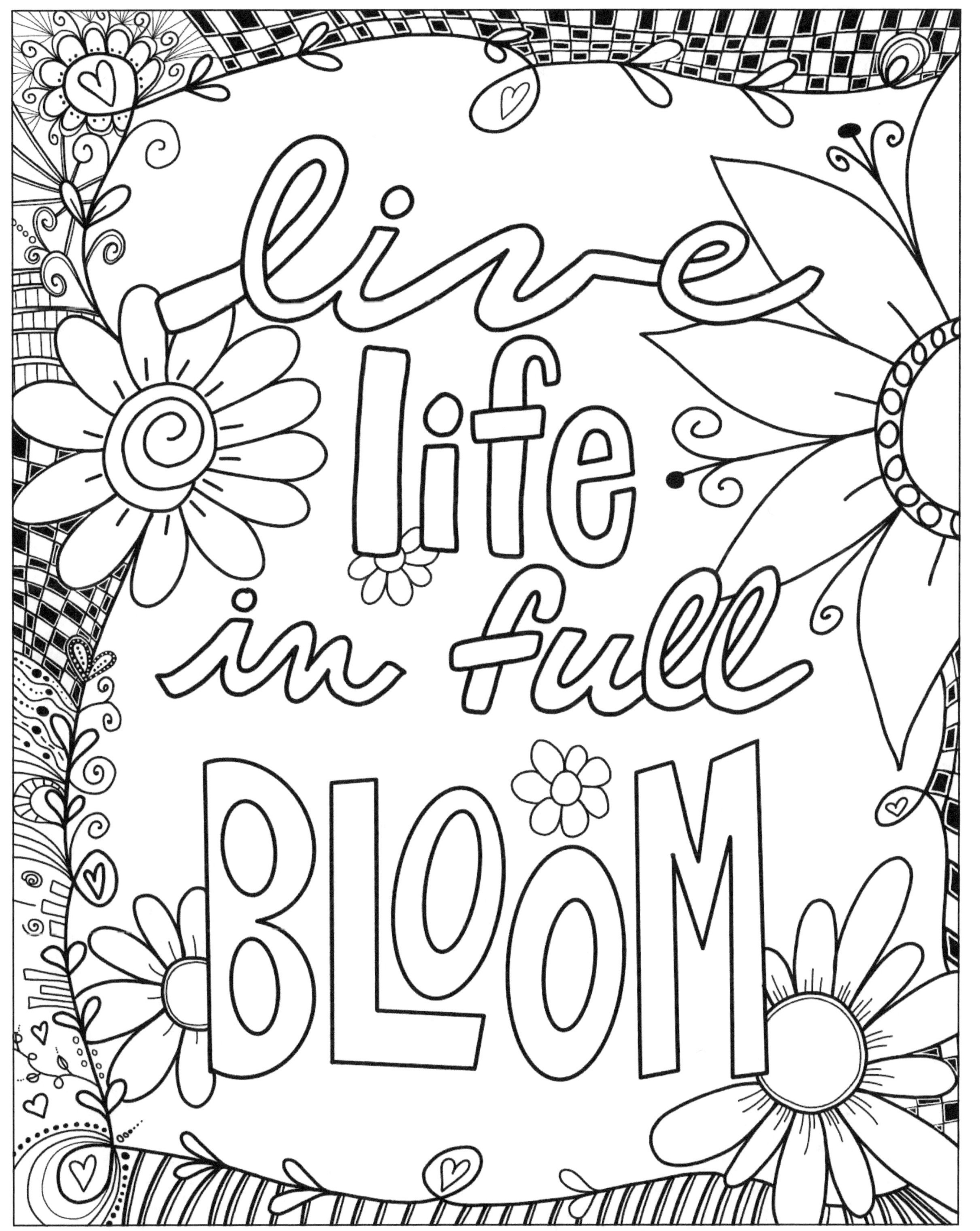

live
life
in full
BLOOM

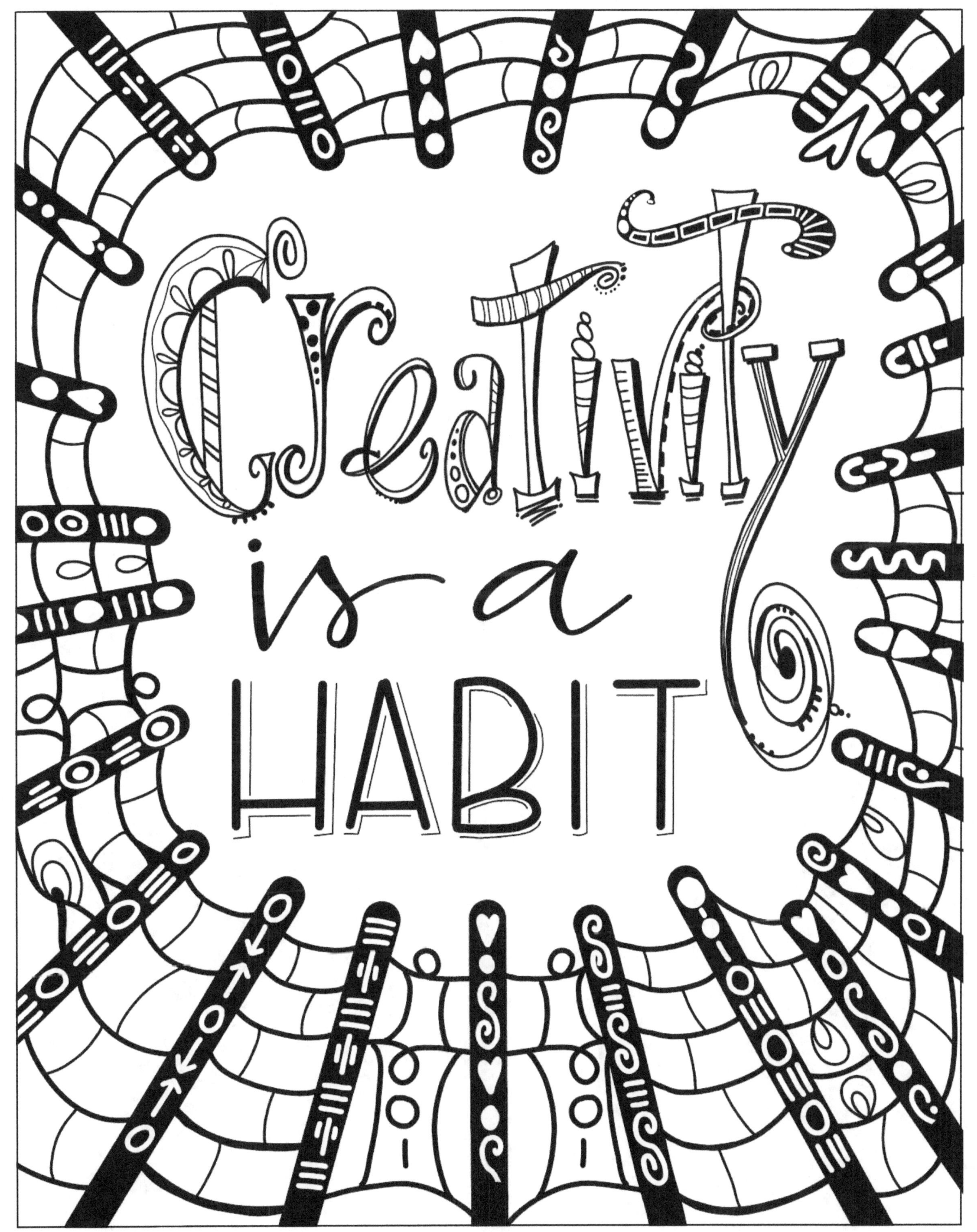

Creativity
is a
HABIT

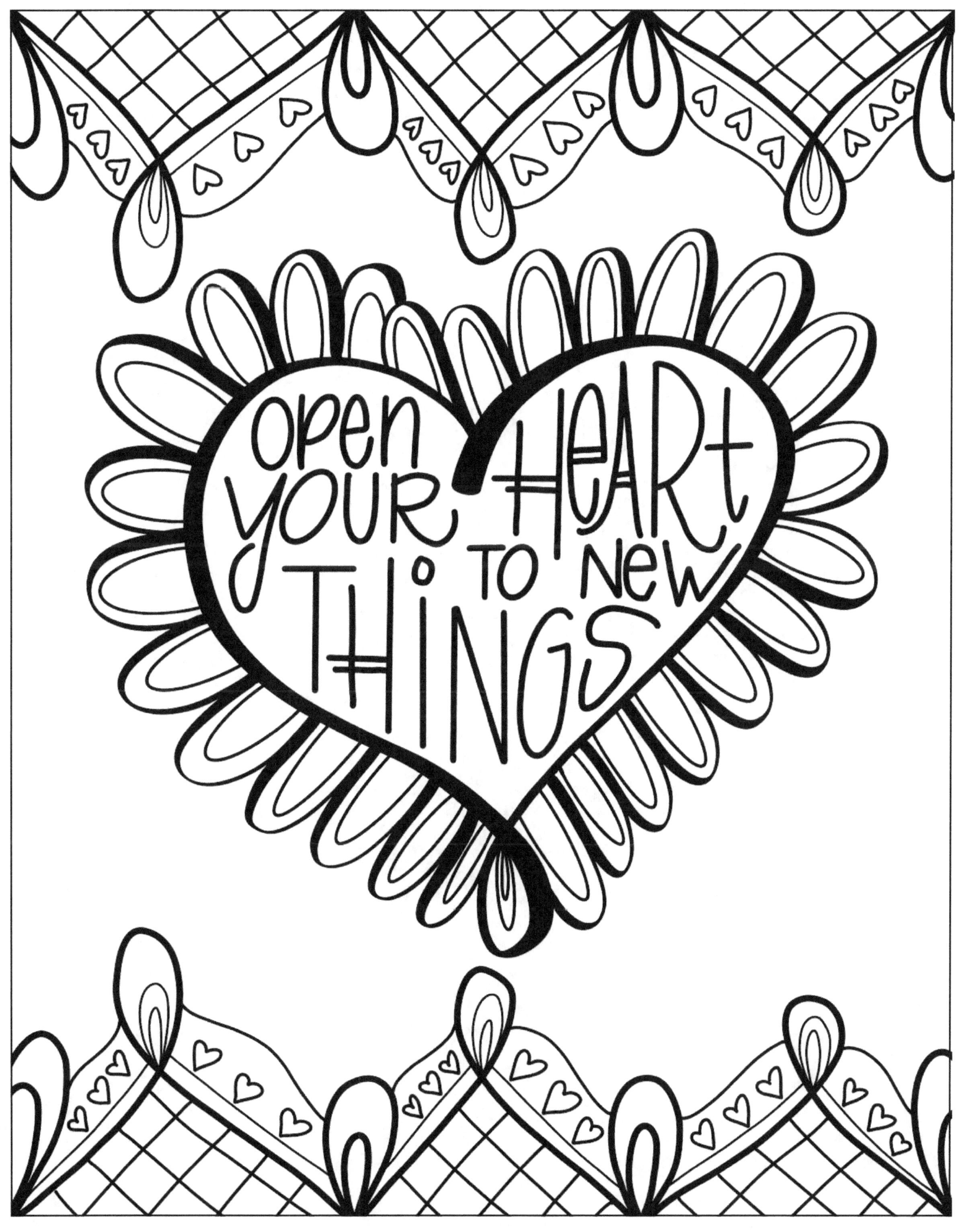

open your HeARt to new THiNGS

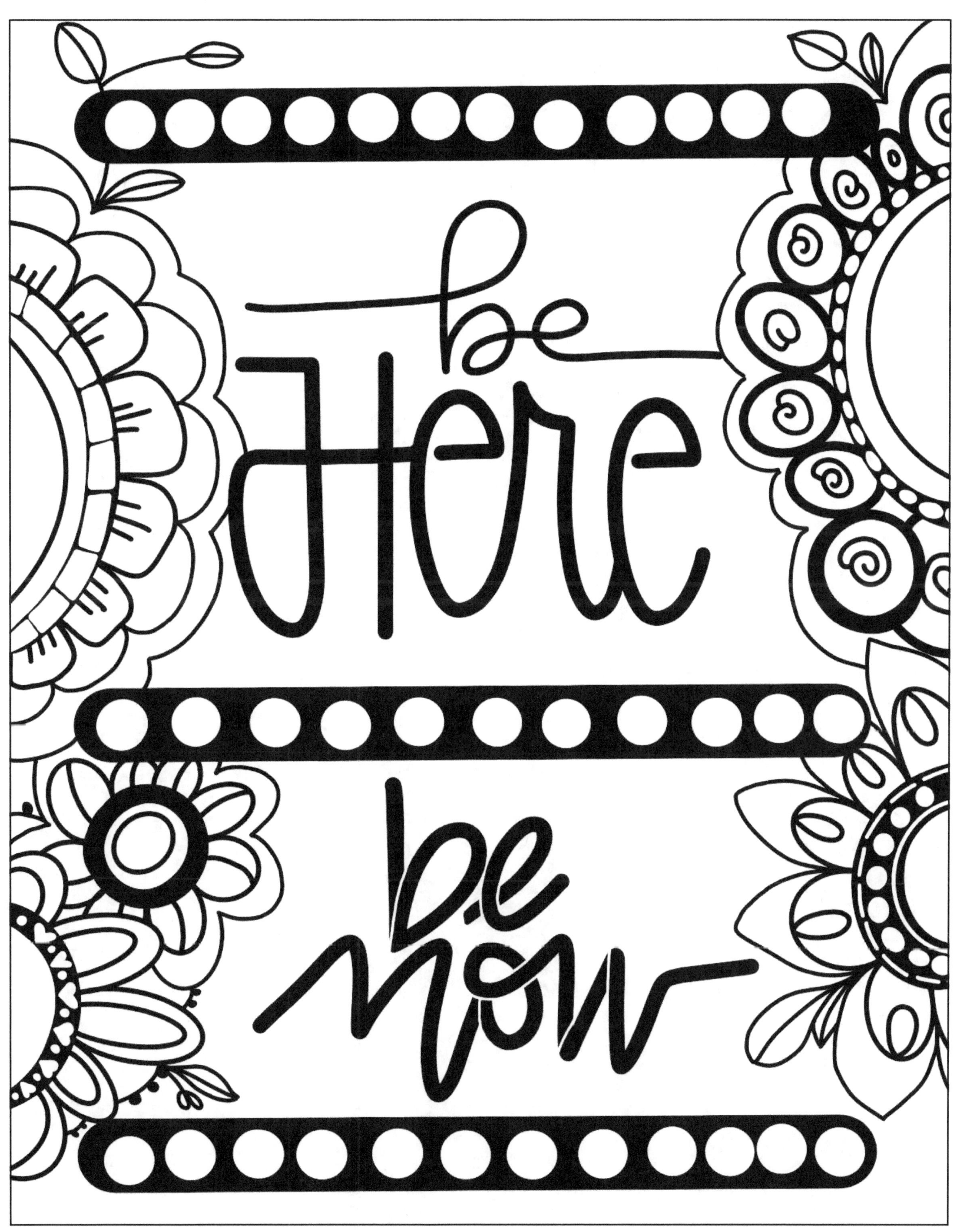

be Here
be now

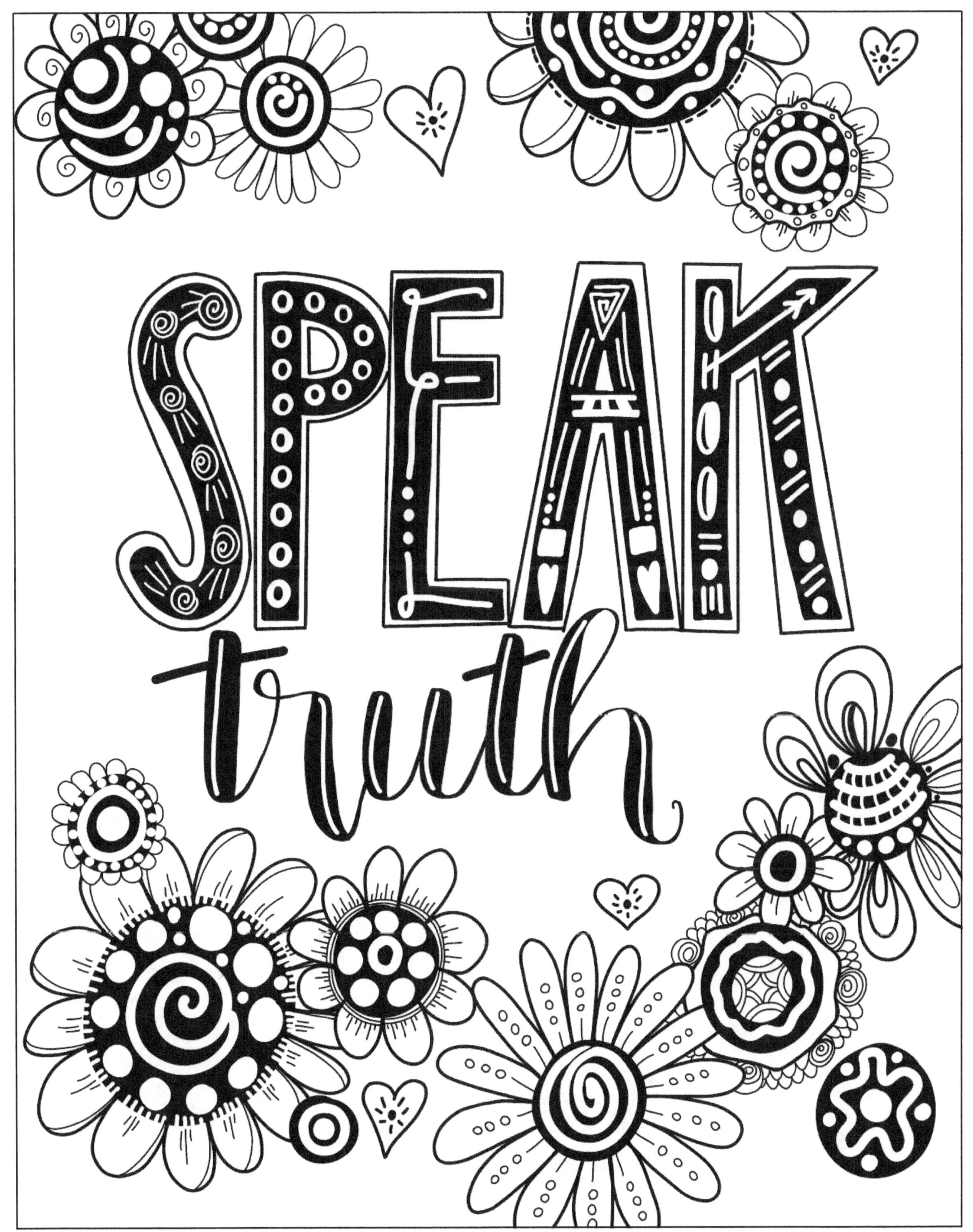

SPEAK
truth

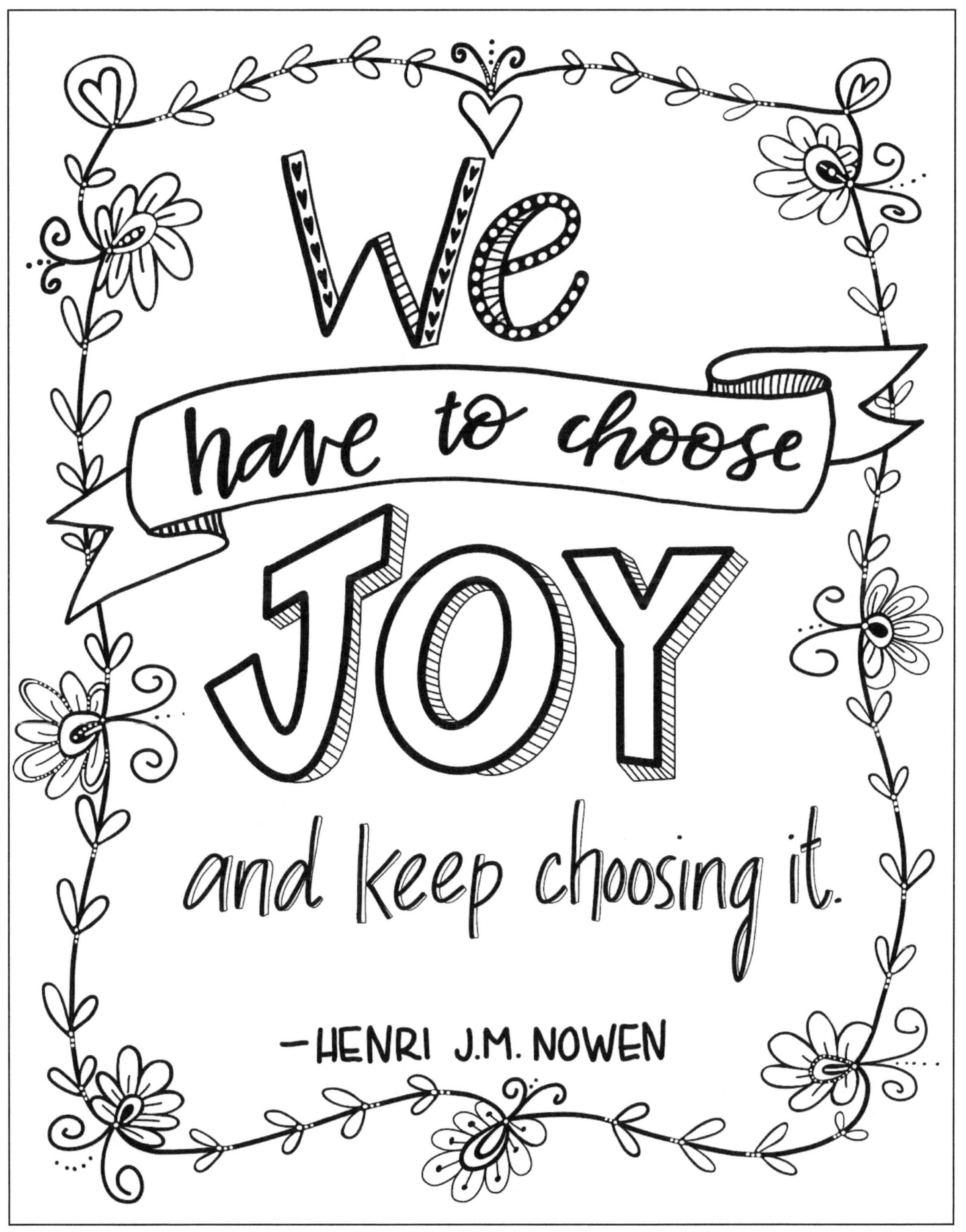
We
have to choose
JOY
and keep choosing it.
-HENRI J.M. NOWEN

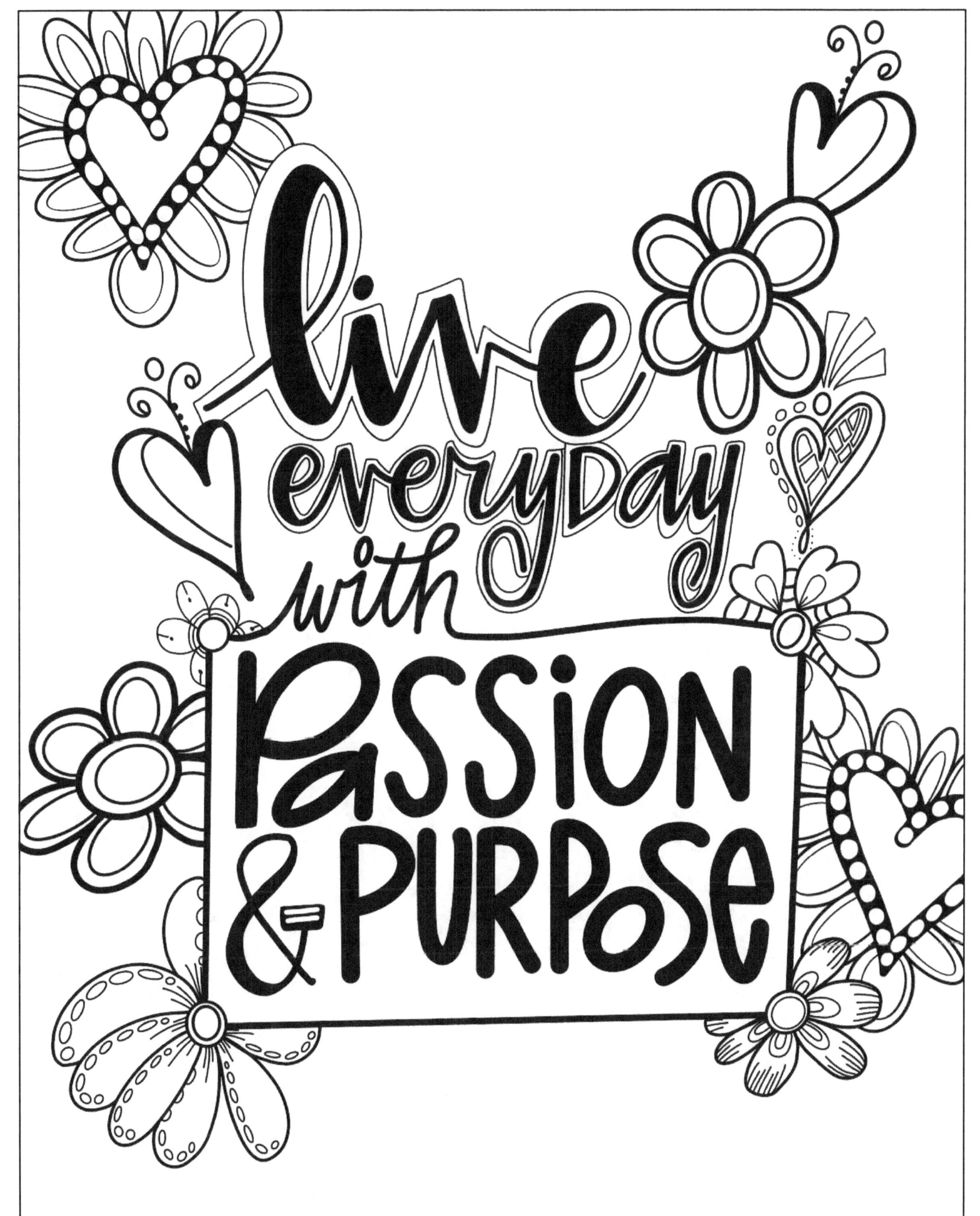

live
everyday
with
passion
& purpose

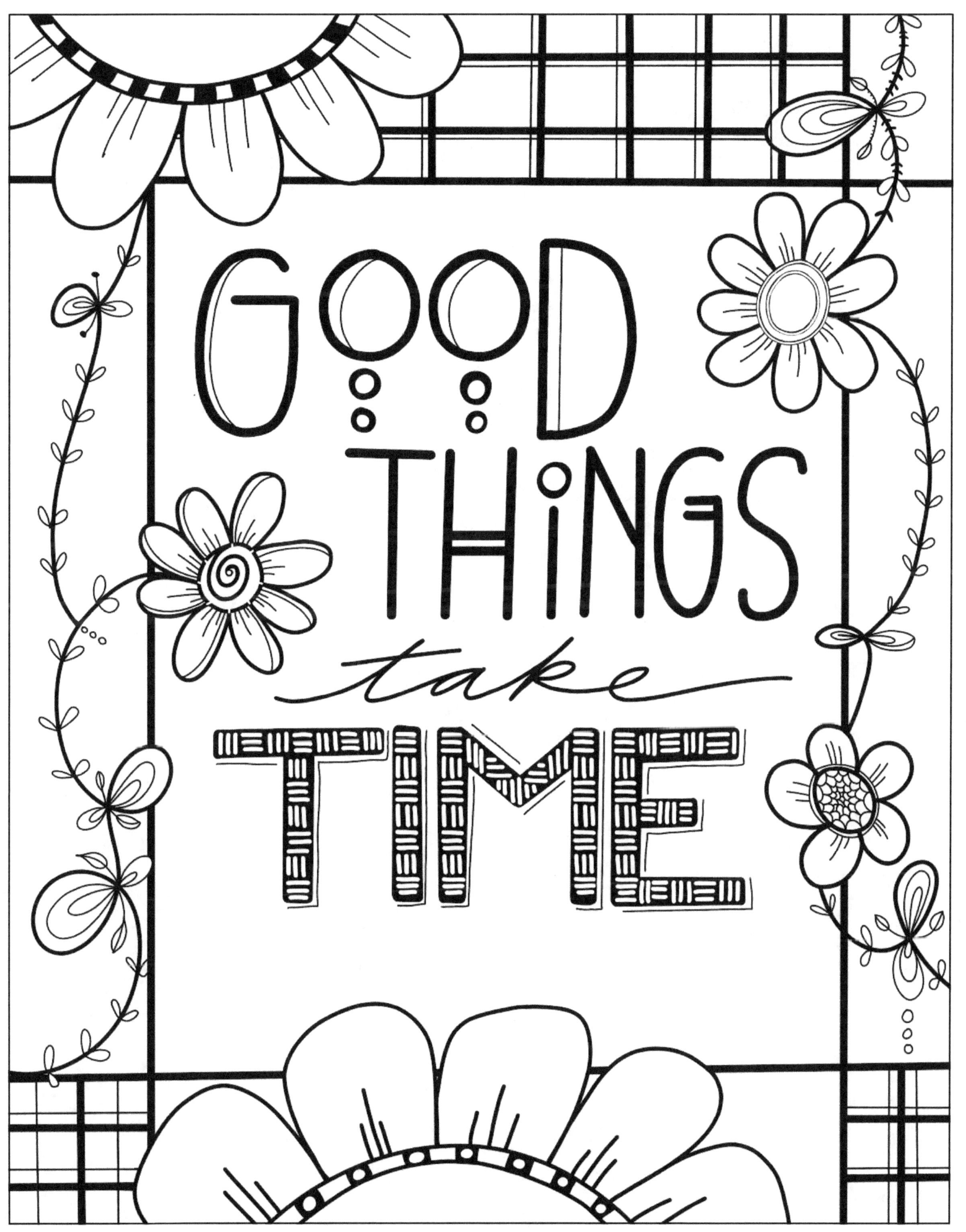

GOOD
THINGS
take
TIME

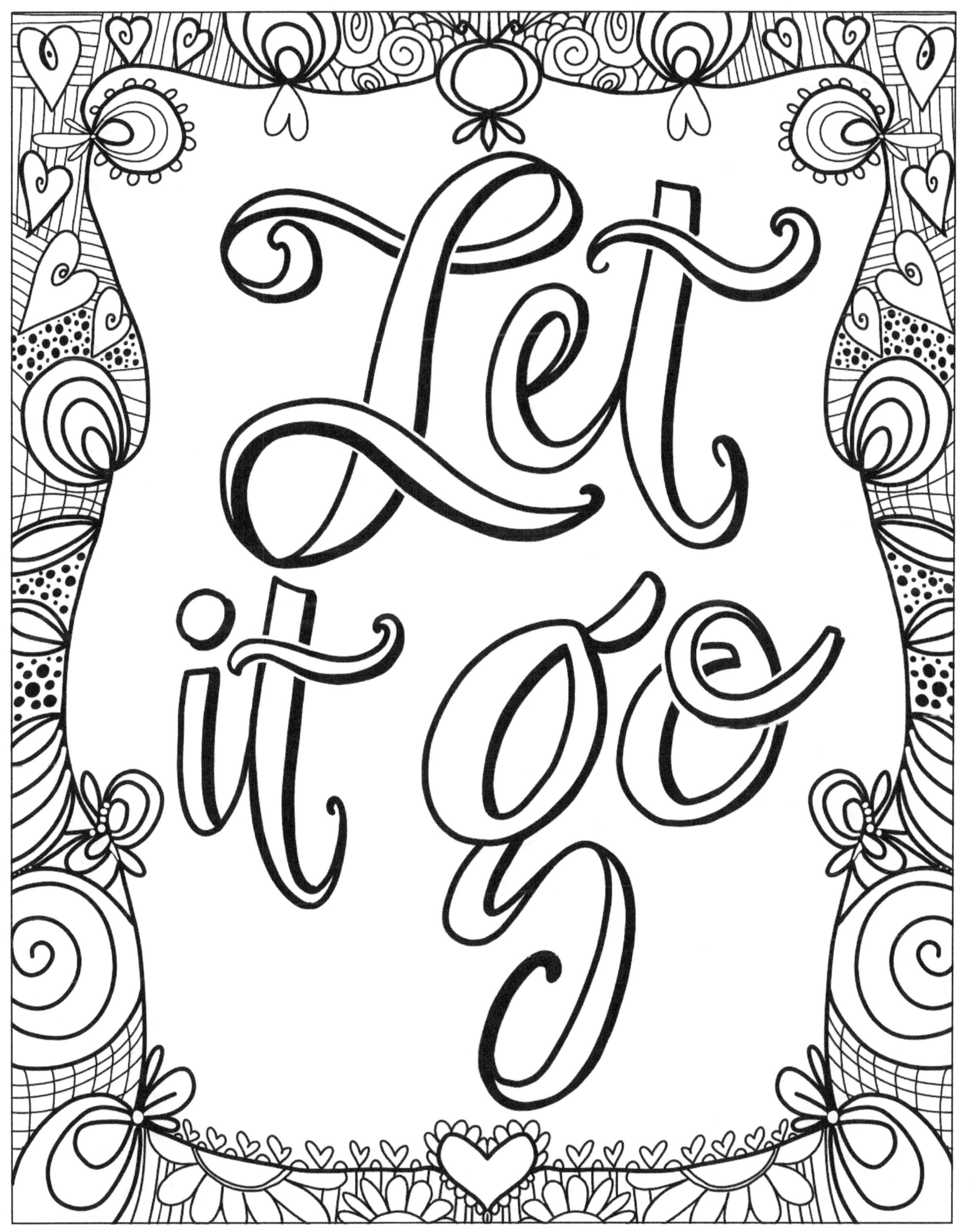

Let
it go

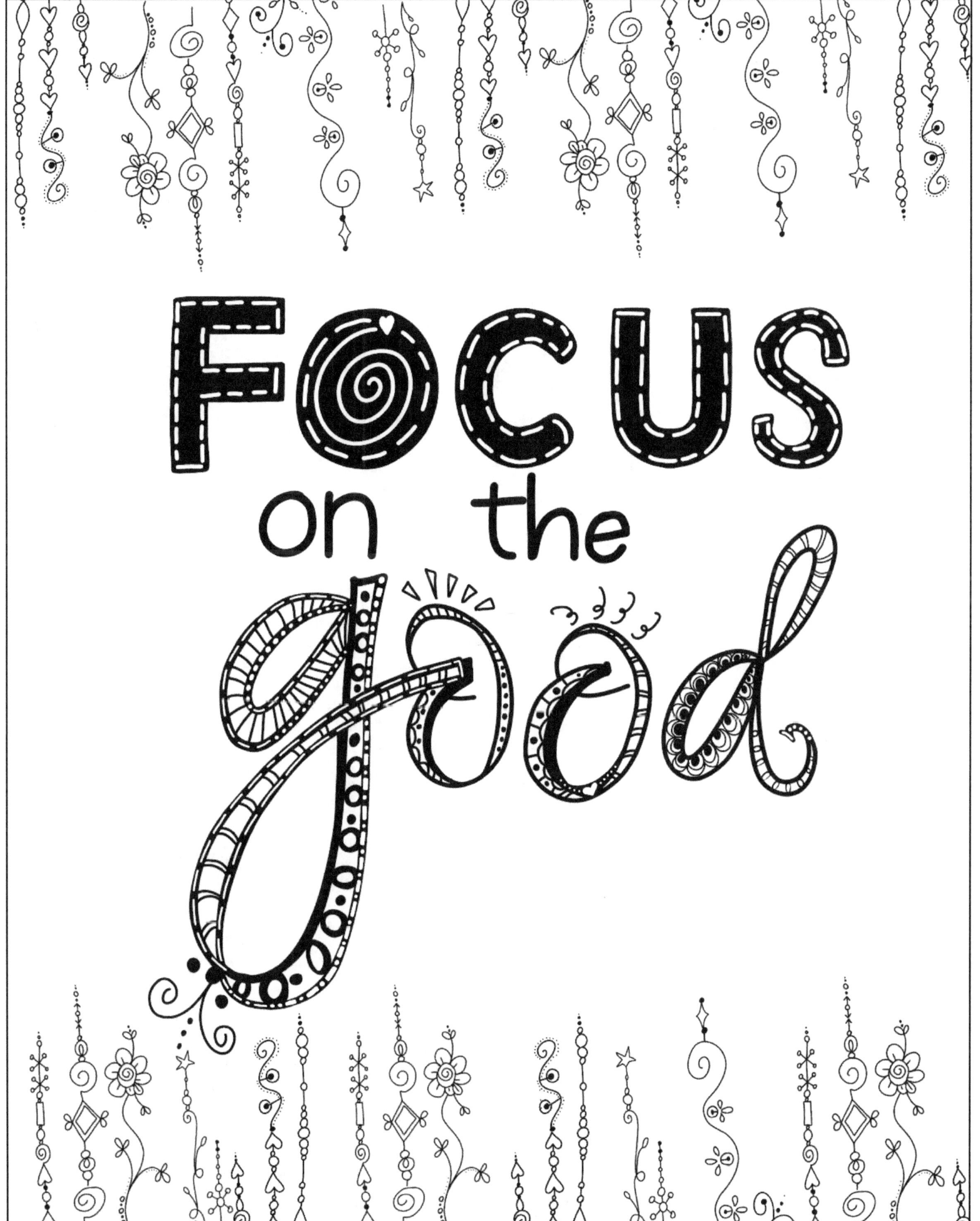

Focus
on the
good

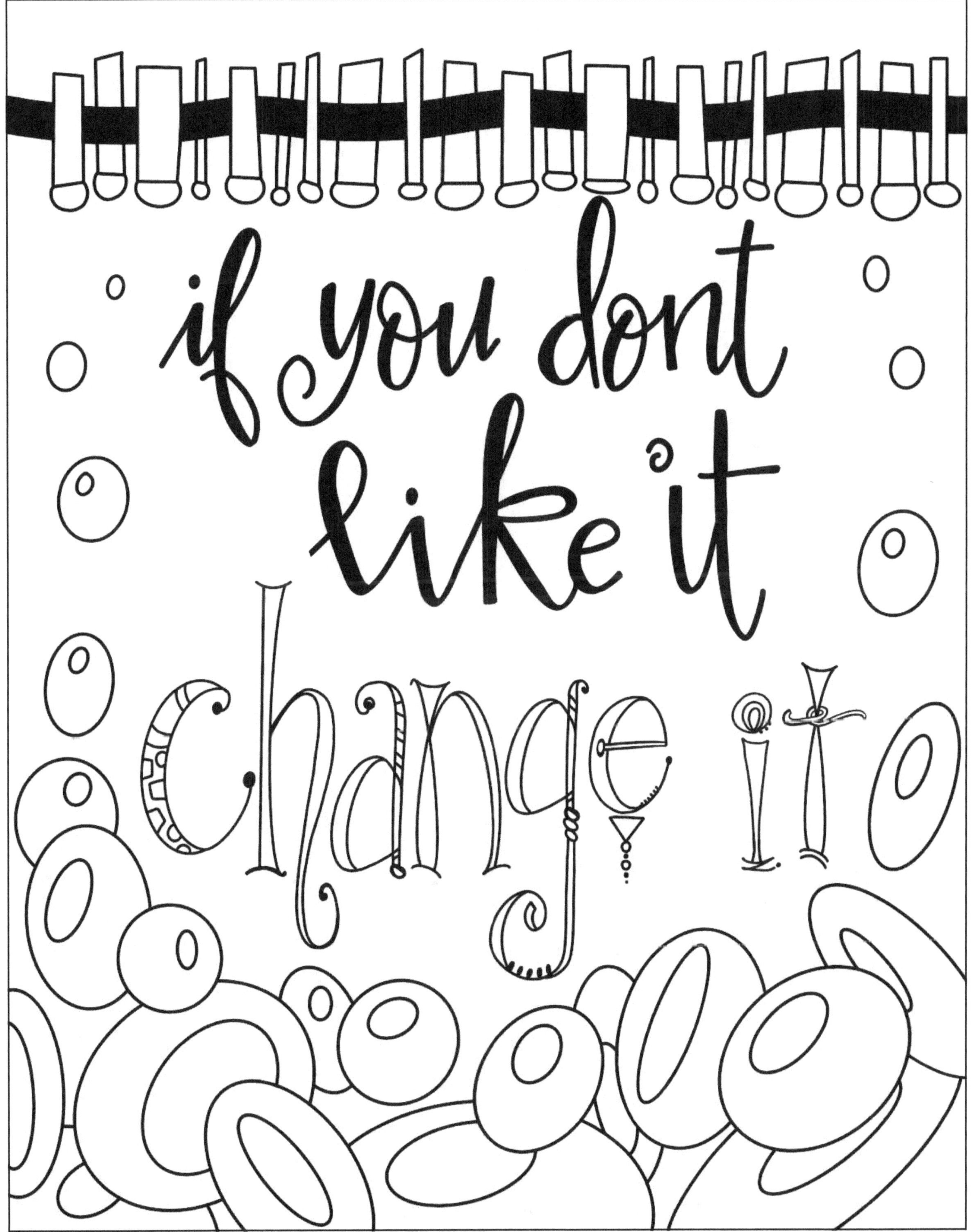

if you dont like it
change it

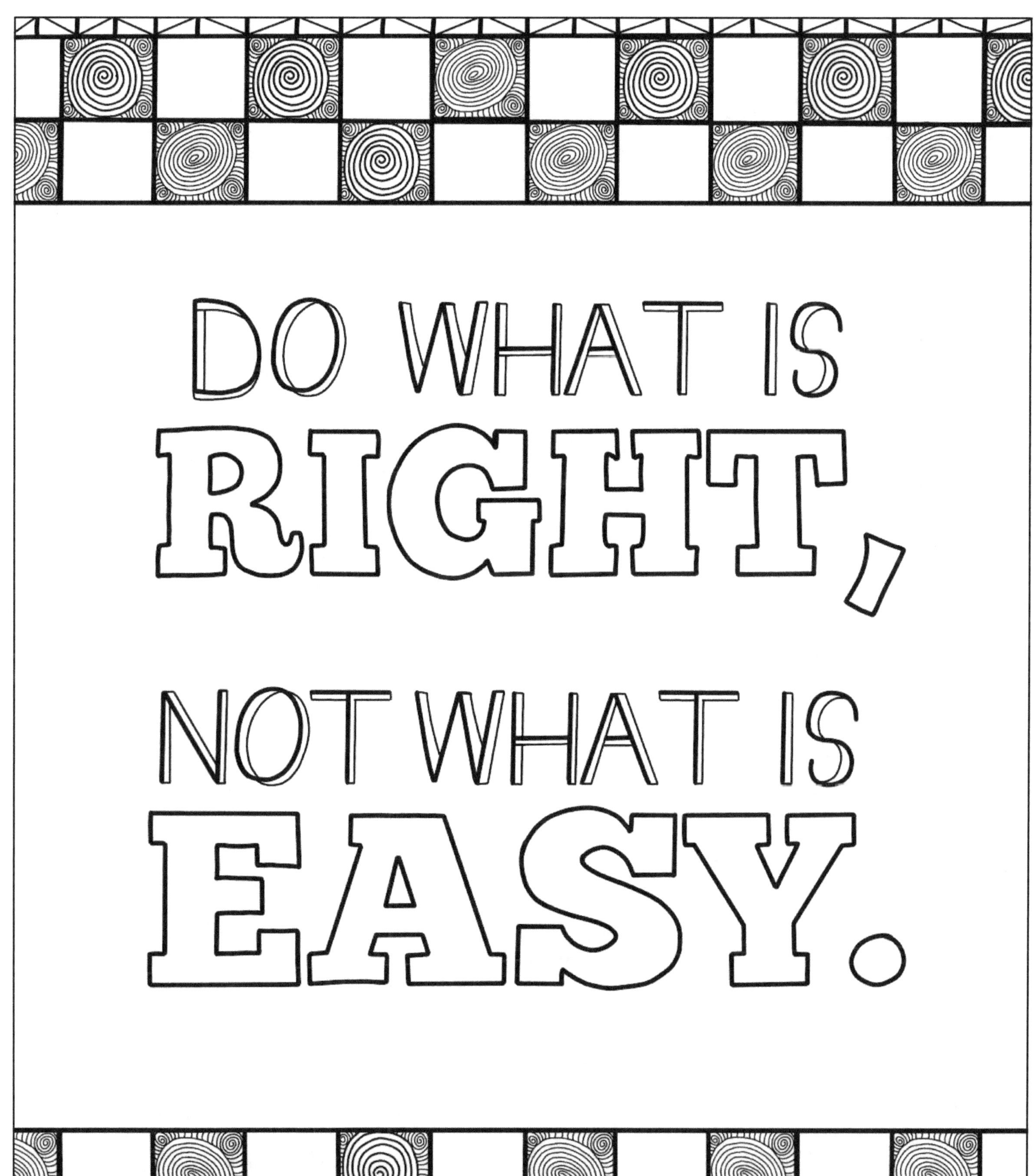

DO WHAT IS
RIGHT,
NOT WHAT IS
EASY.
© 2018 Super Doodle Girl

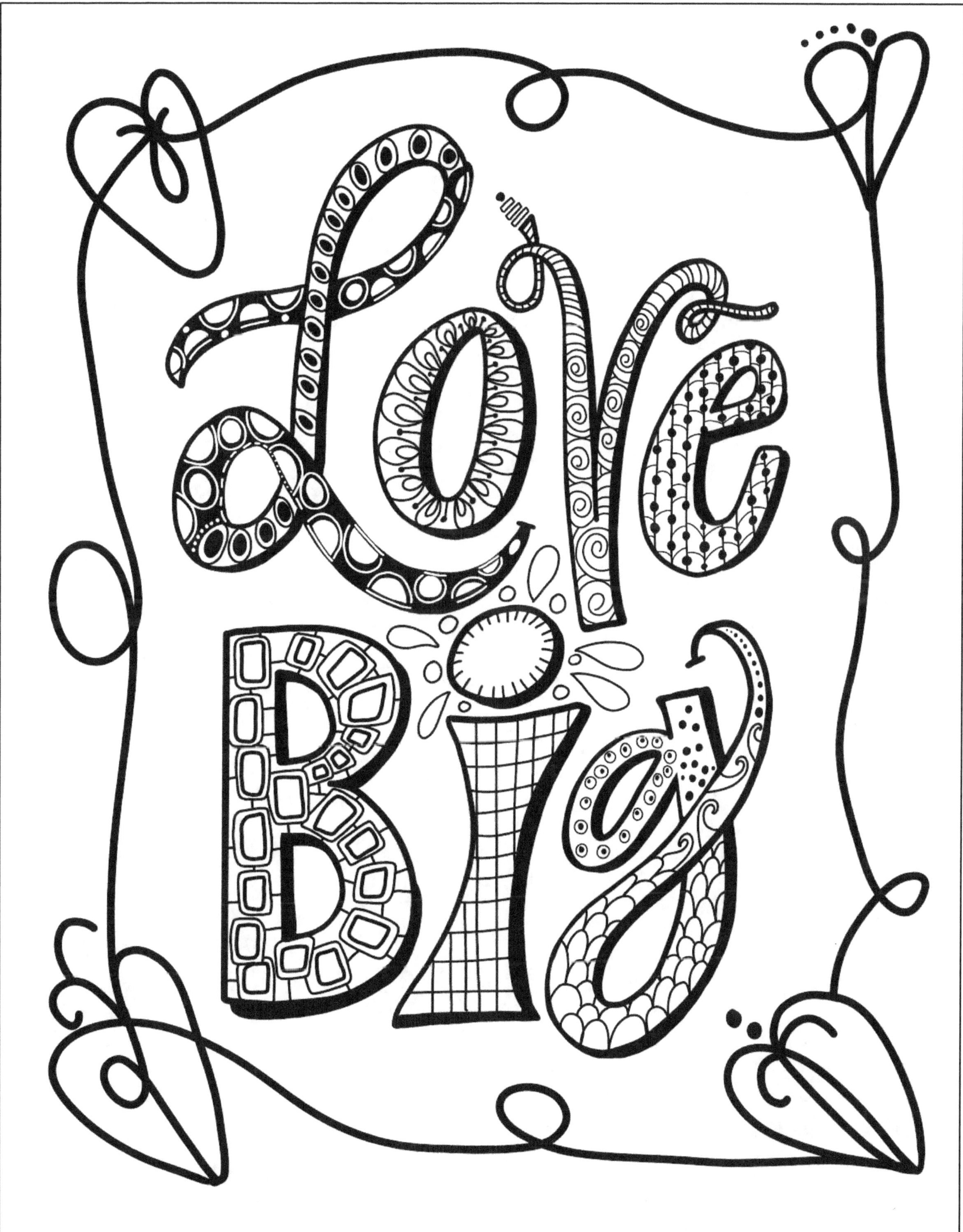

Love
Big

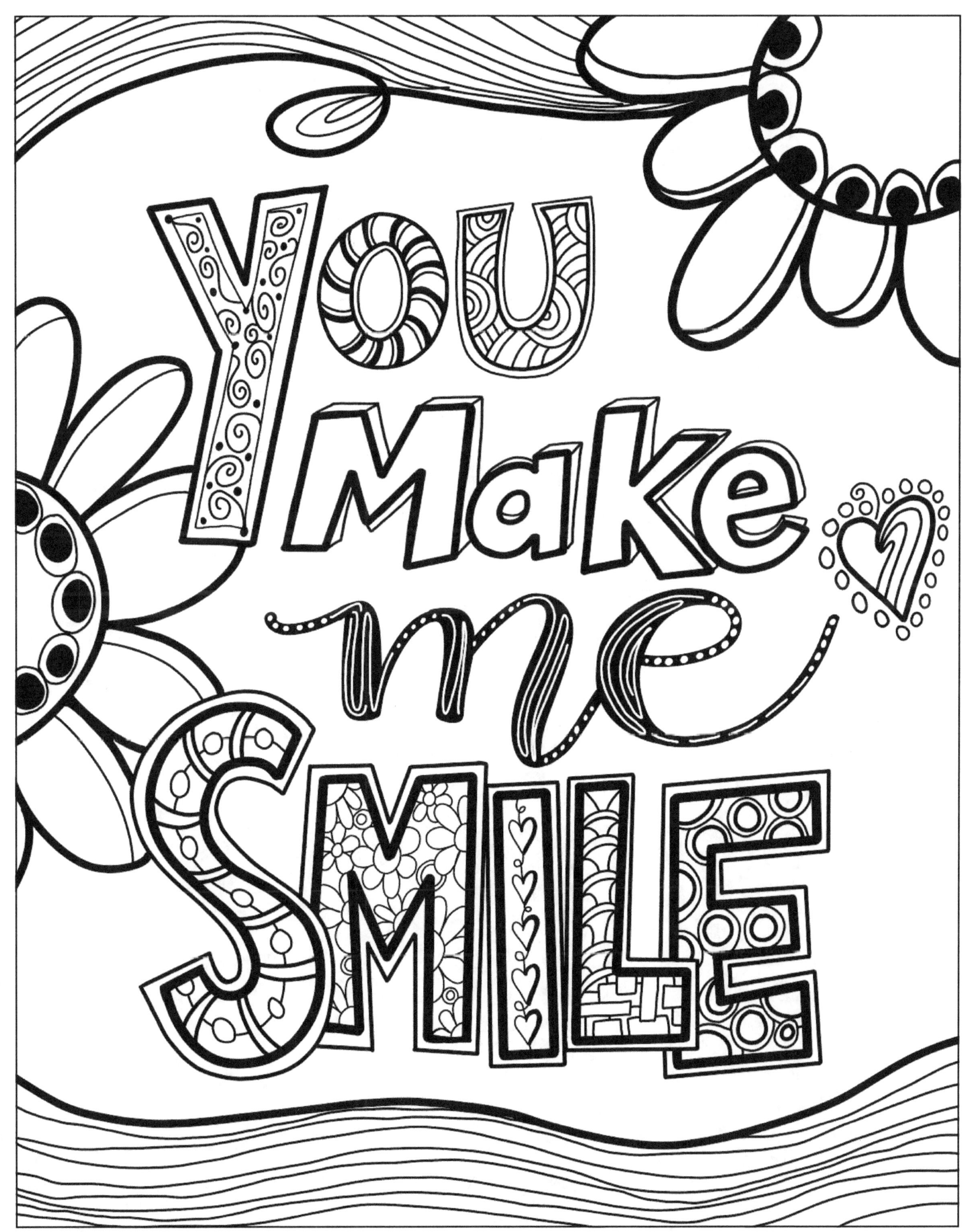

You Make me SMILE

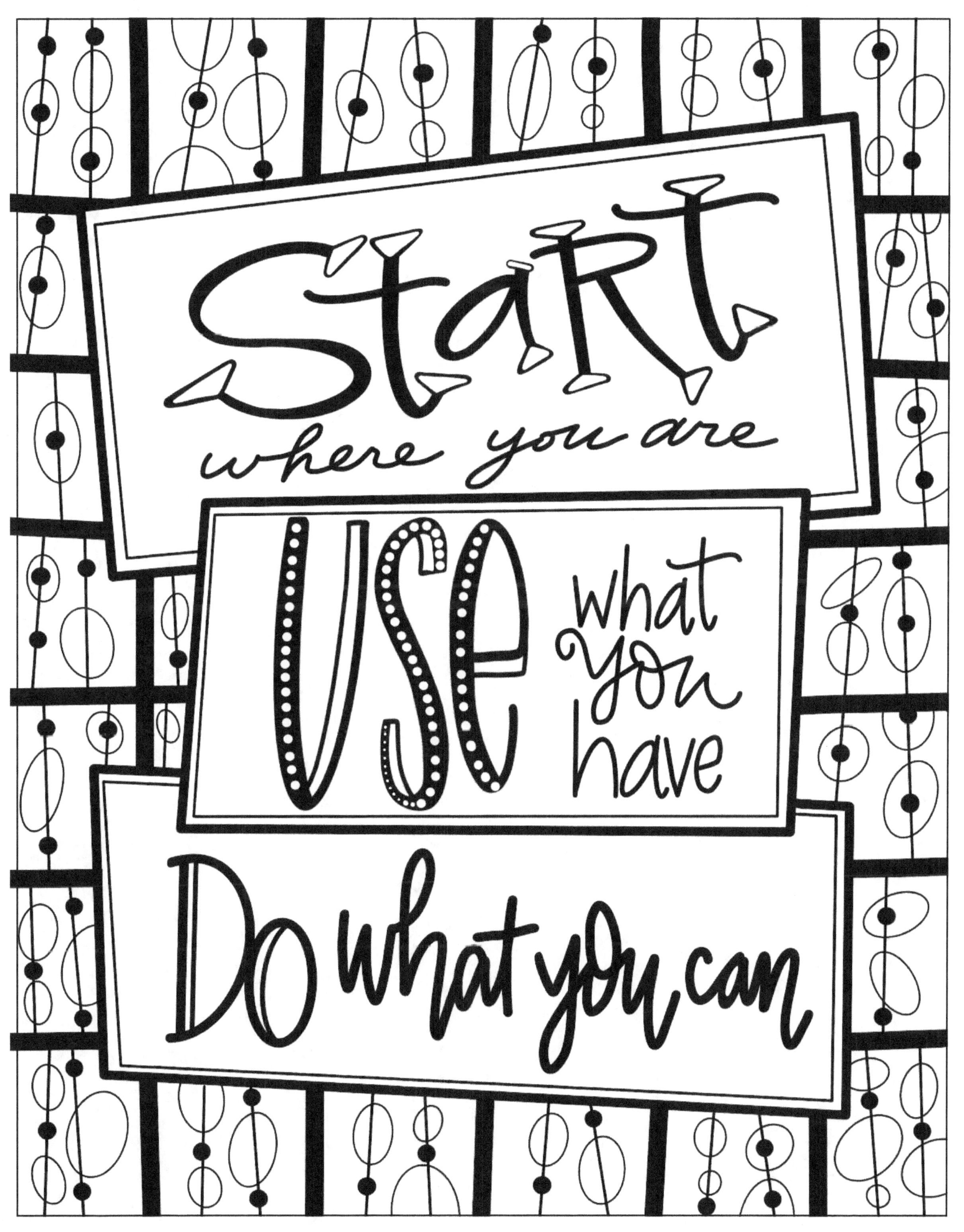

Start where you are
Use what you have
Do what you can

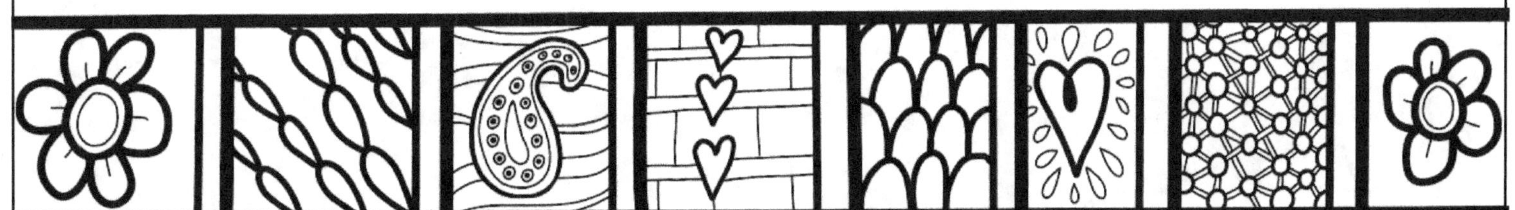

# MAKE TODAY AMAZING

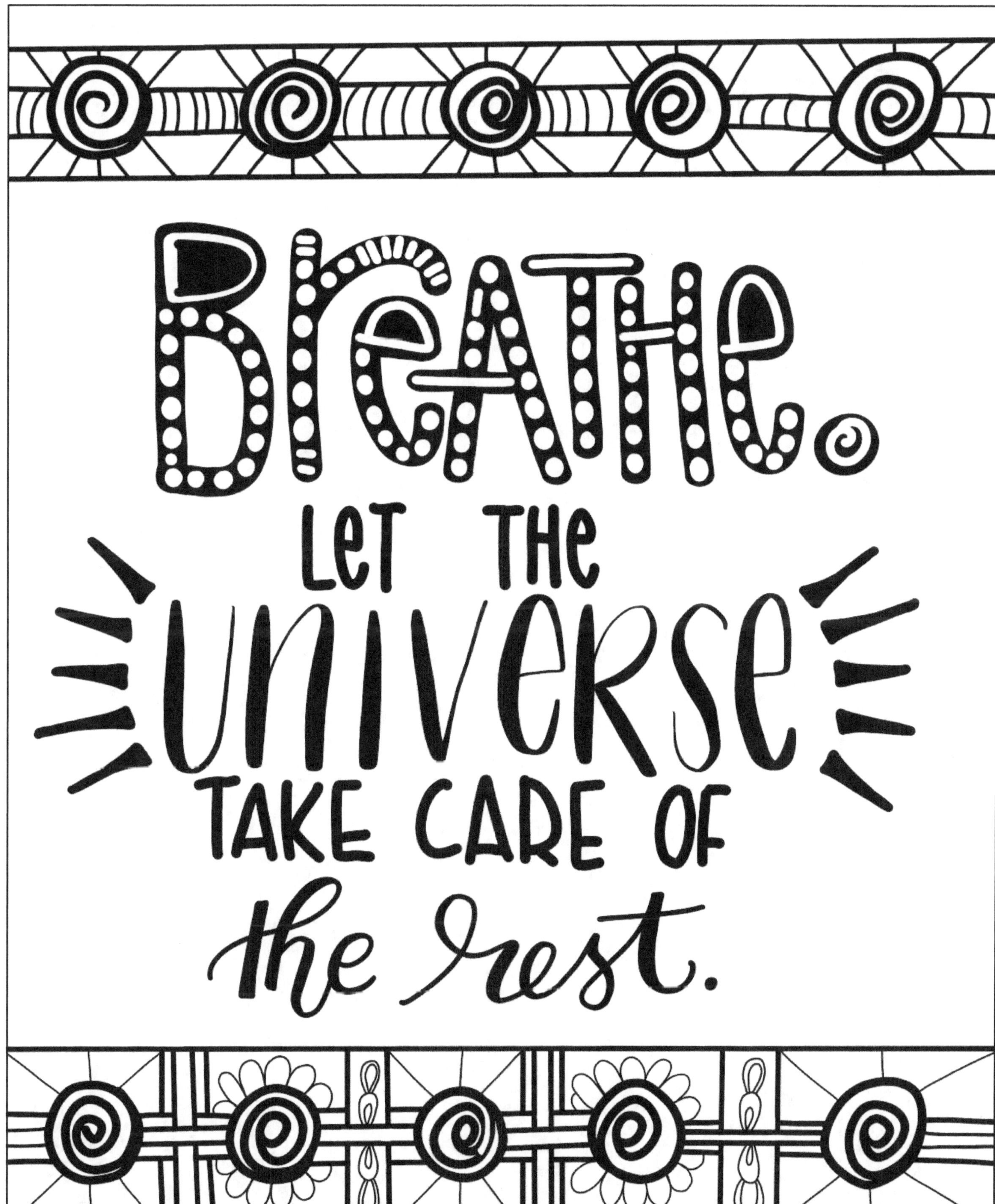

Breathe.
Let the
universe
take care of
the rest.

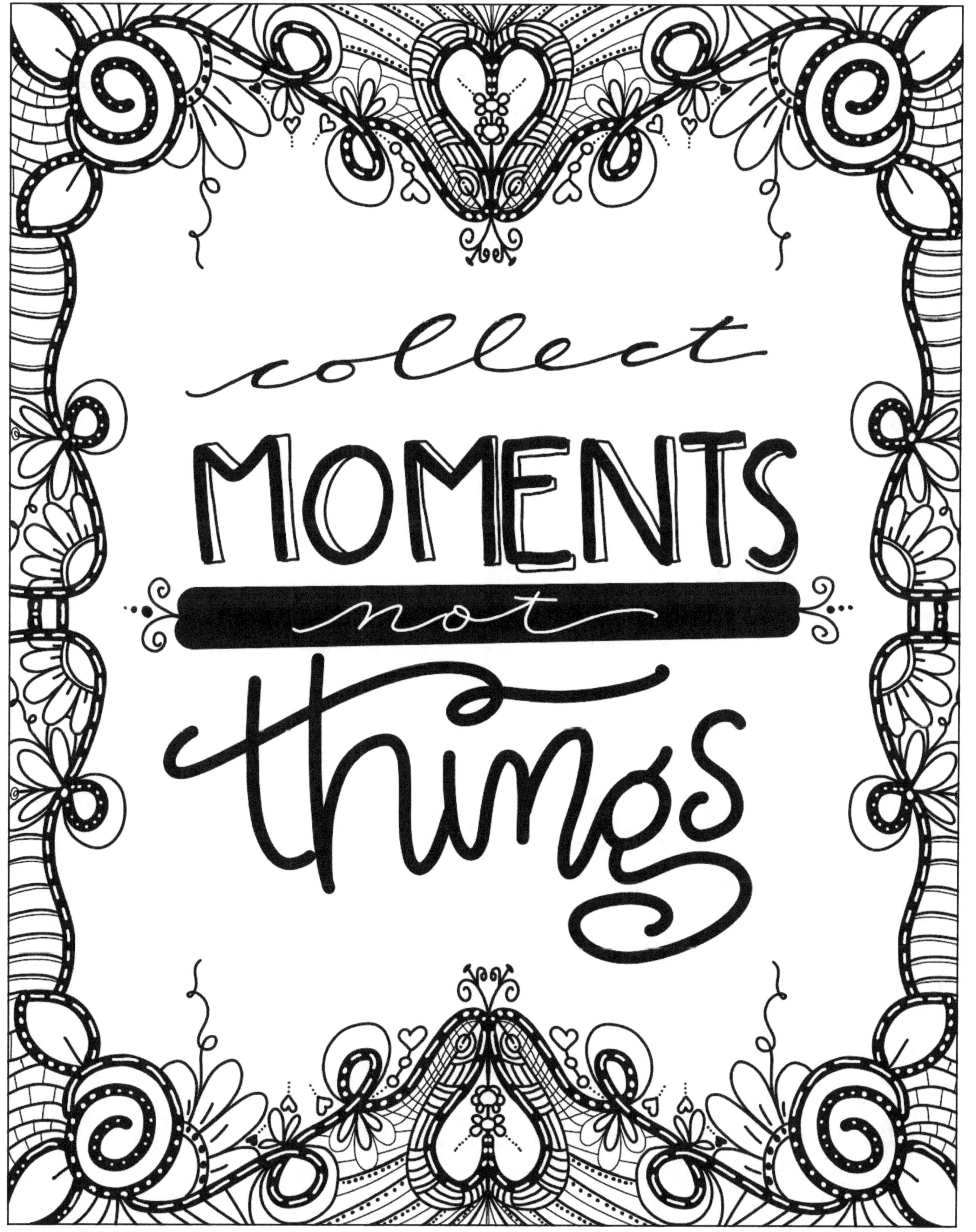

collect
MOMENTS
not
things

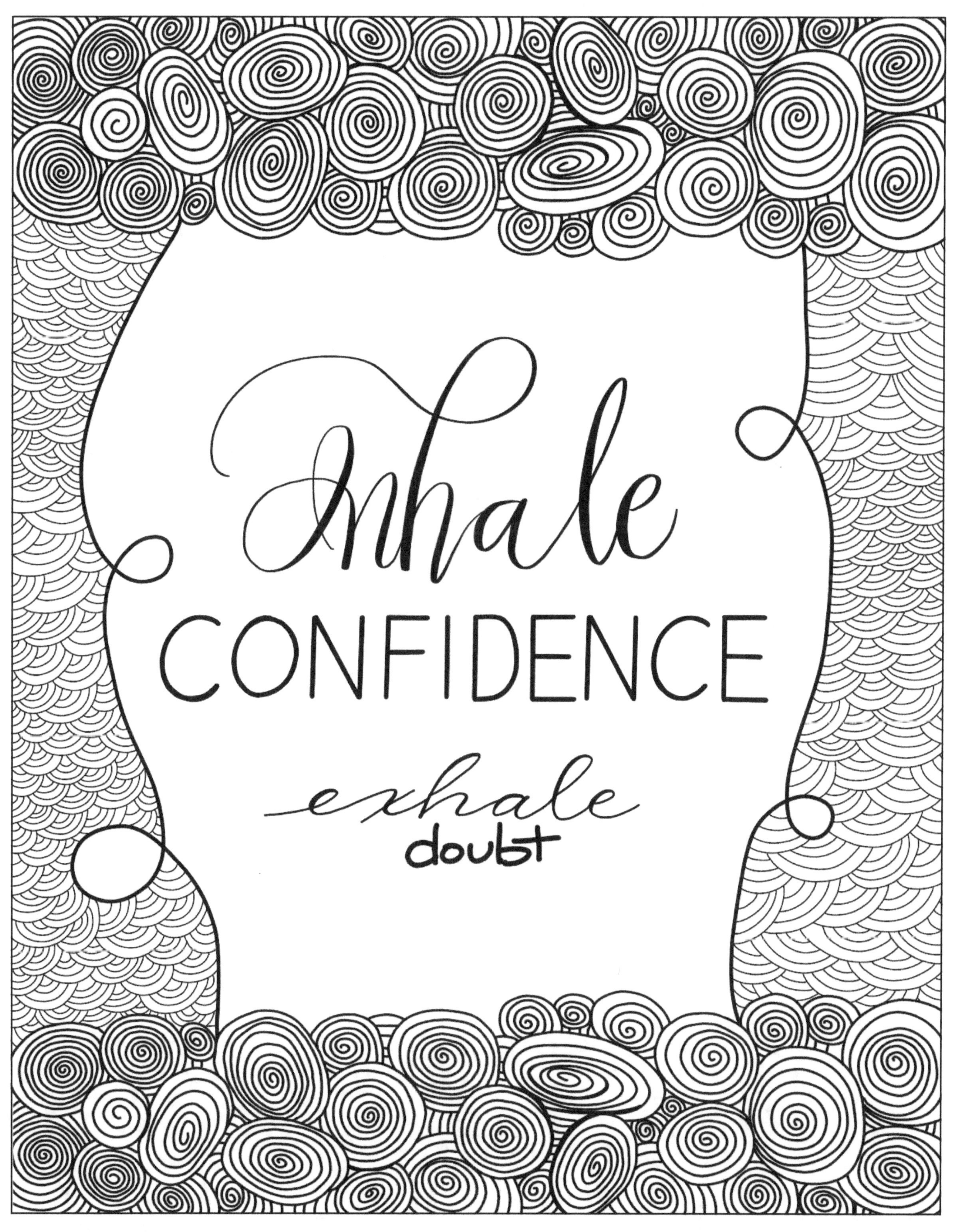

Inhale
CONFIDENCE
exhale
doubt

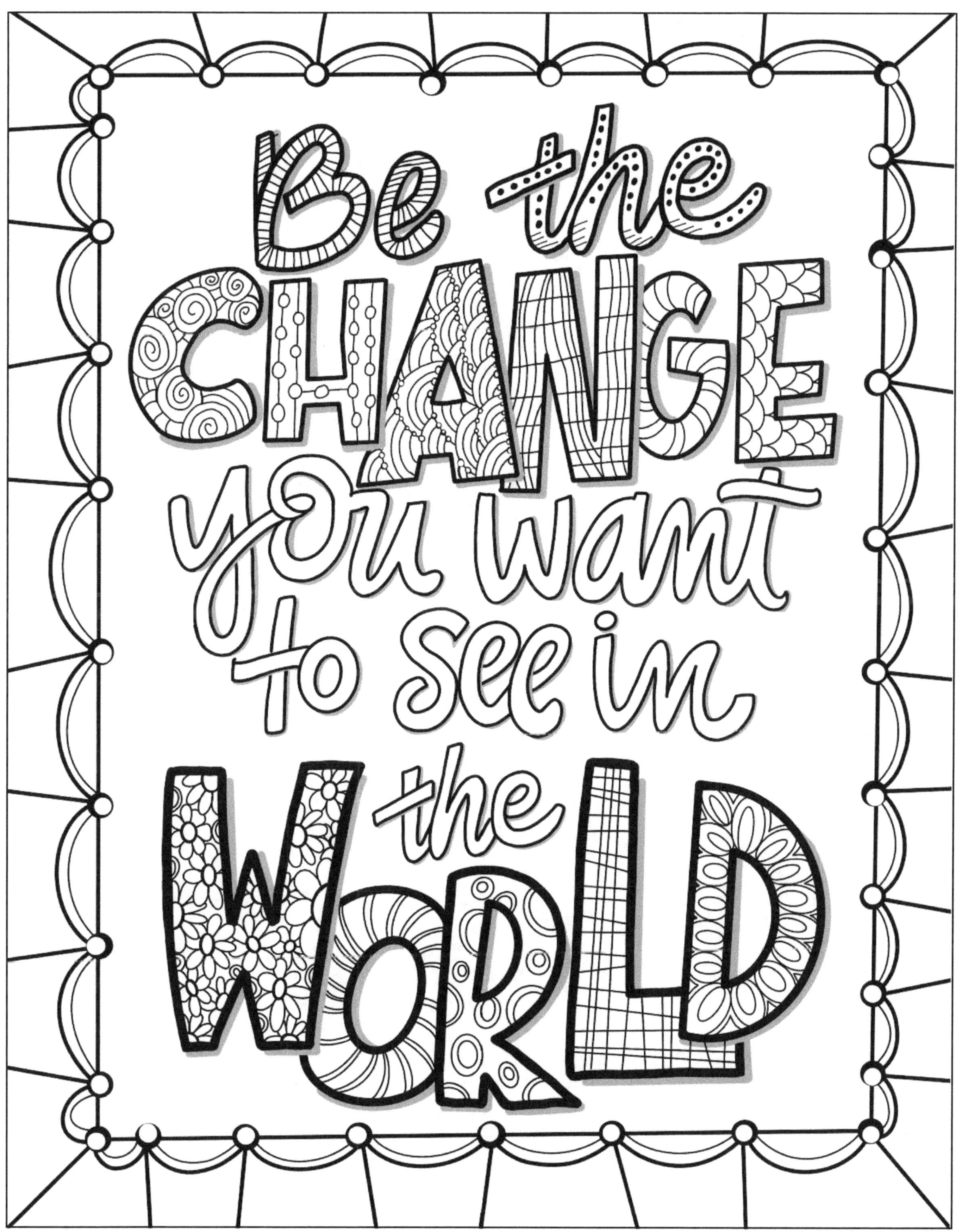

Be the
CHANGE
you want
to see in
the
WORLD

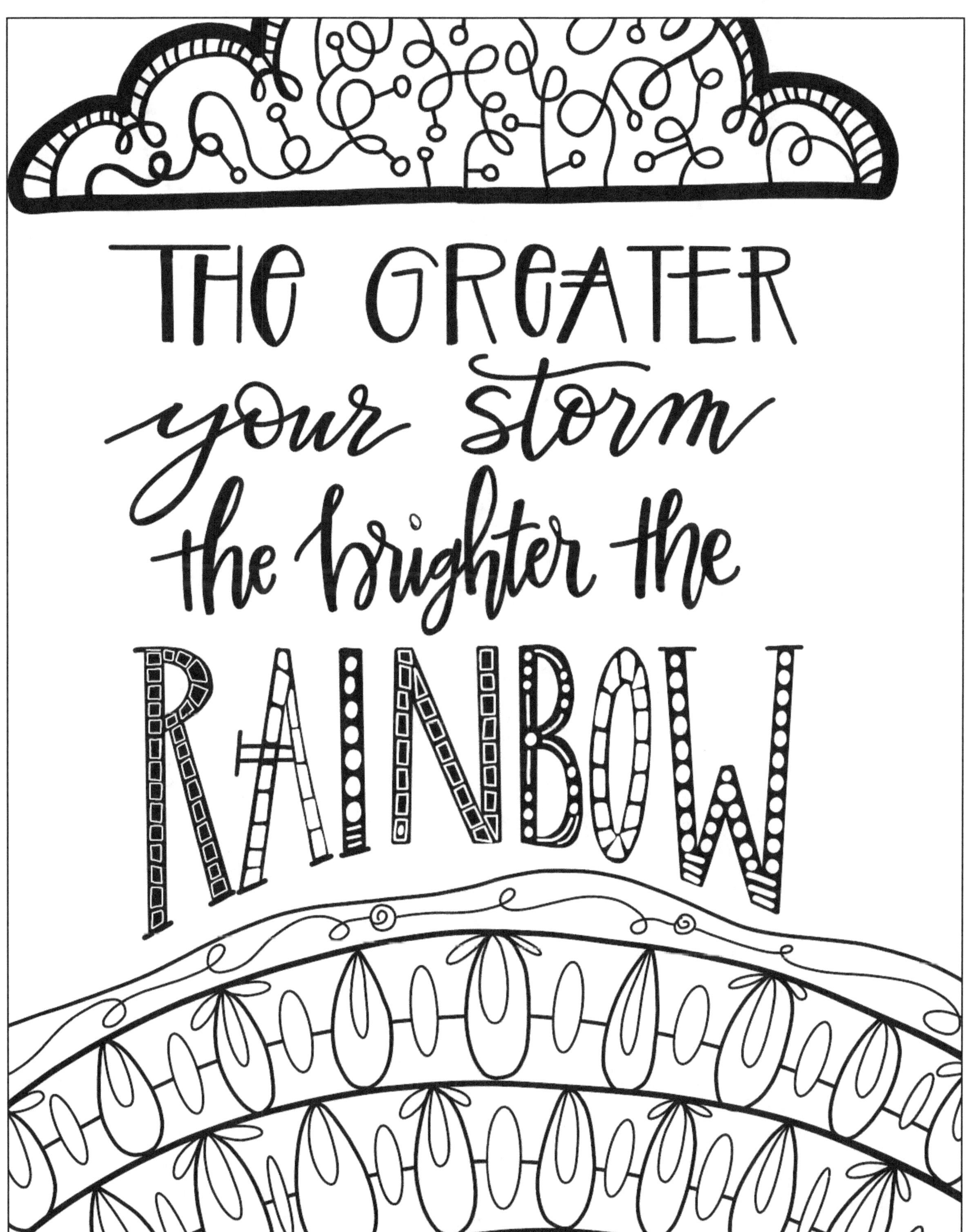

THE GREATER
your storm
the brighter the
RAINBOW

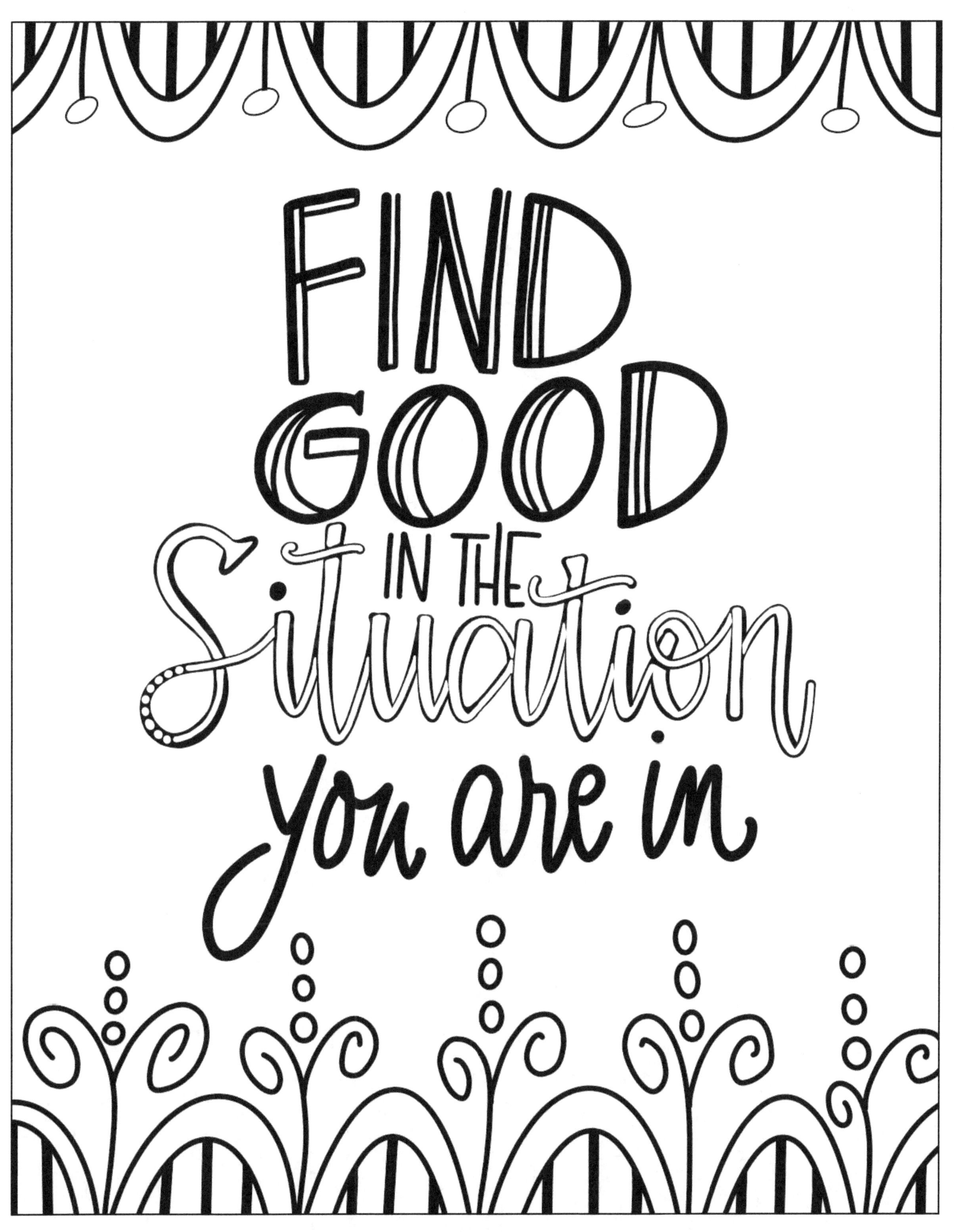

FIND
GOOD
IN THE
Situation
you are in

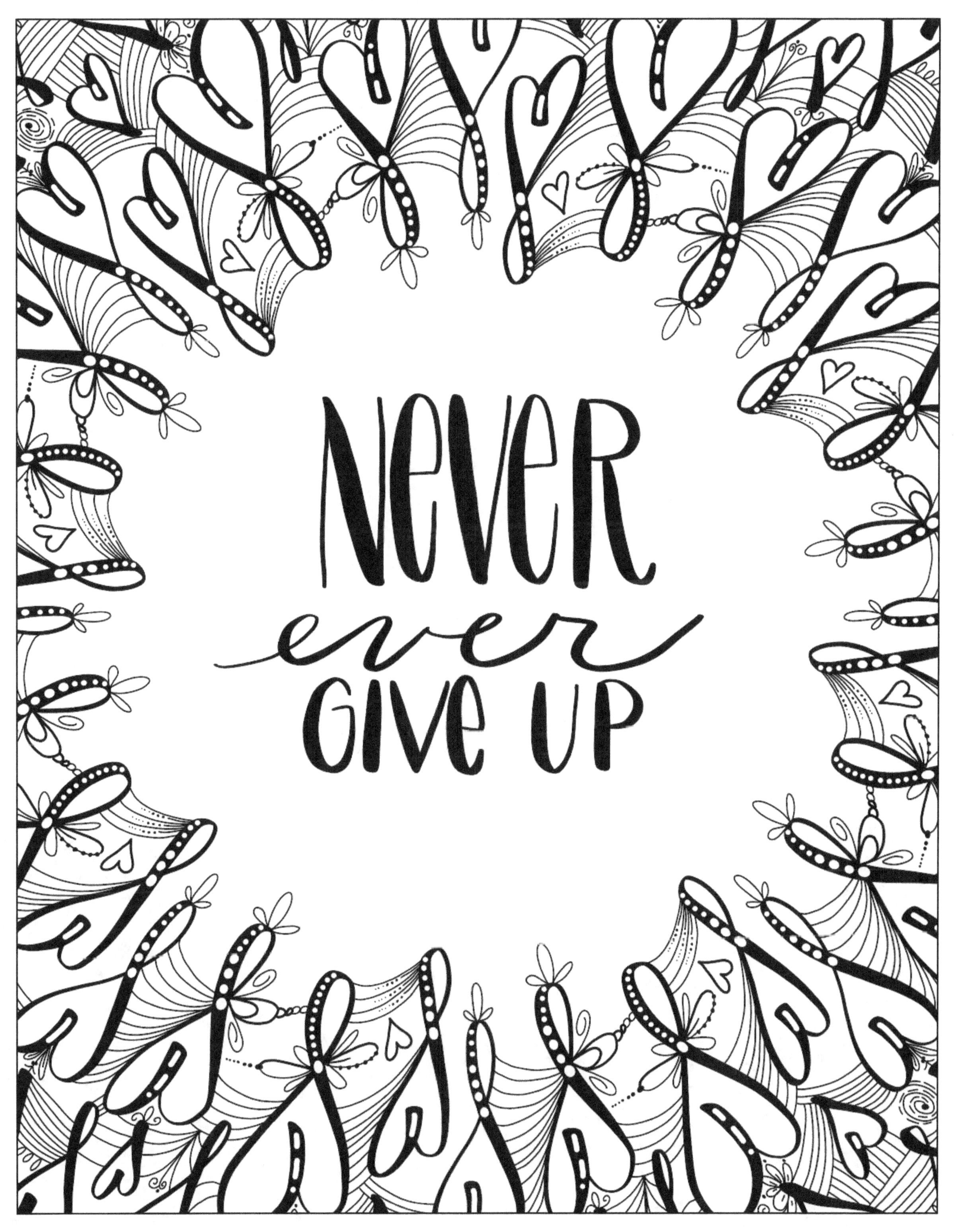

NEVER
ever
GIVE UP

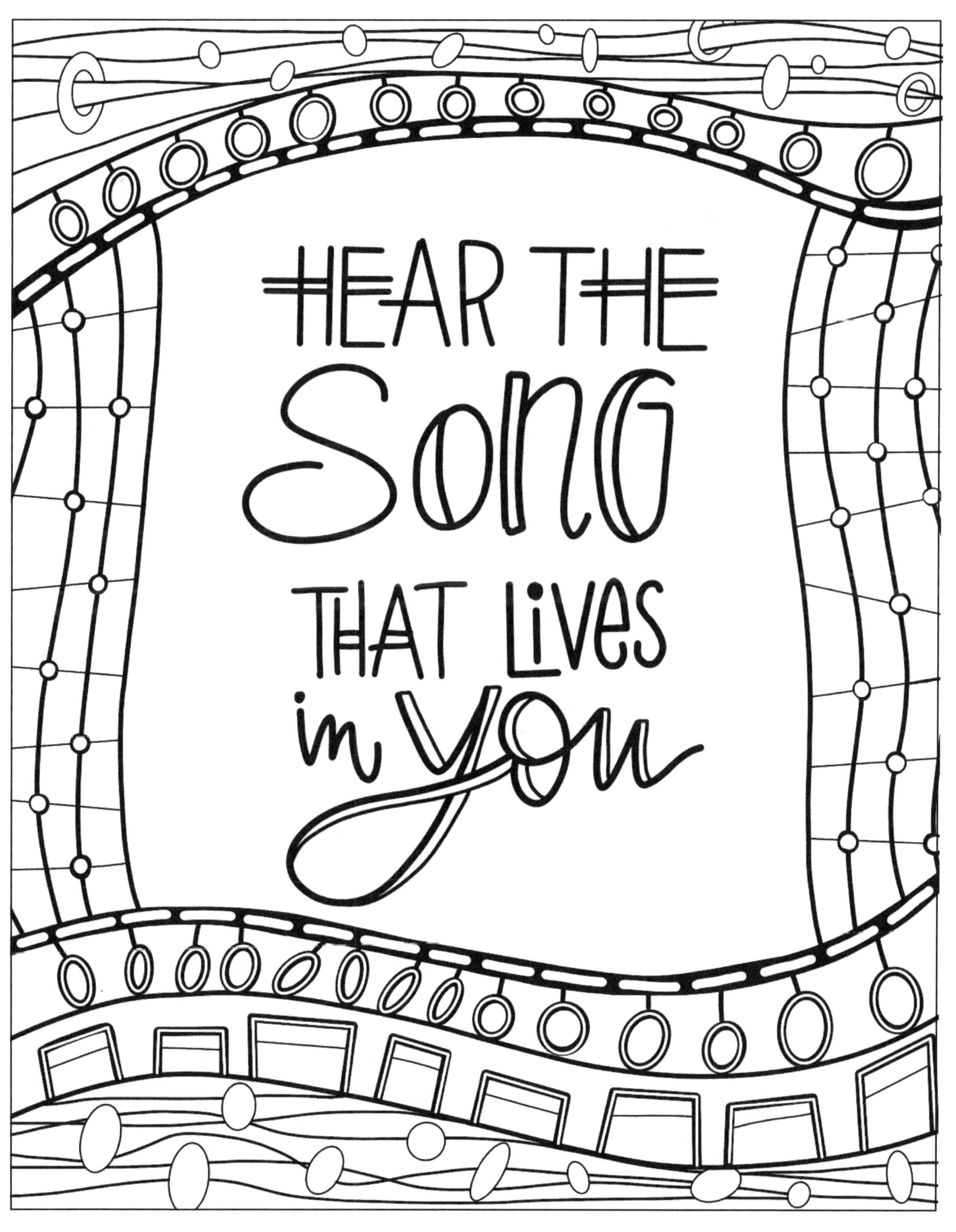

HEAR THE
SONG
THAT LIVES
in YOU

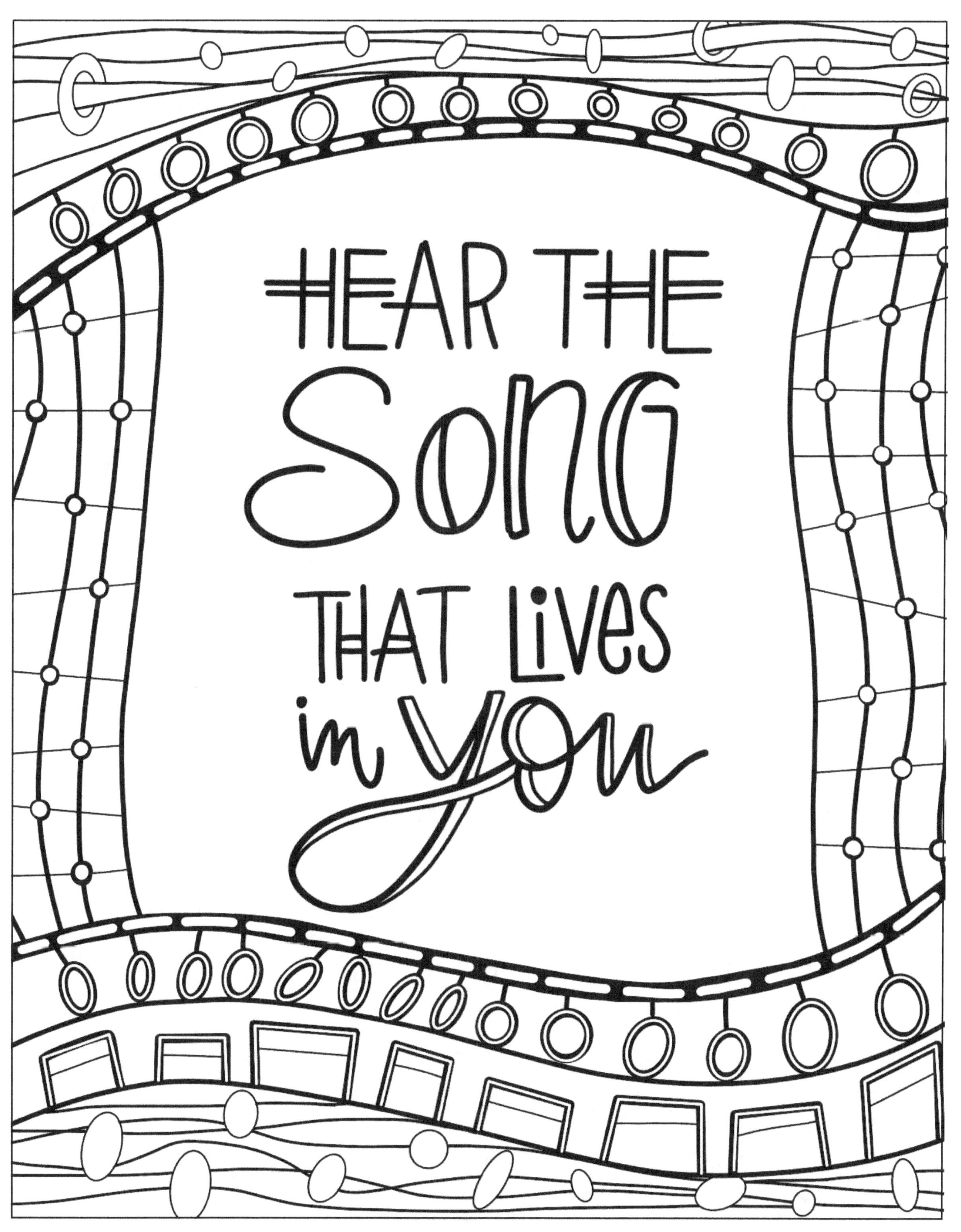

HEAR THE
SONG
THAT LIVES
in YOU

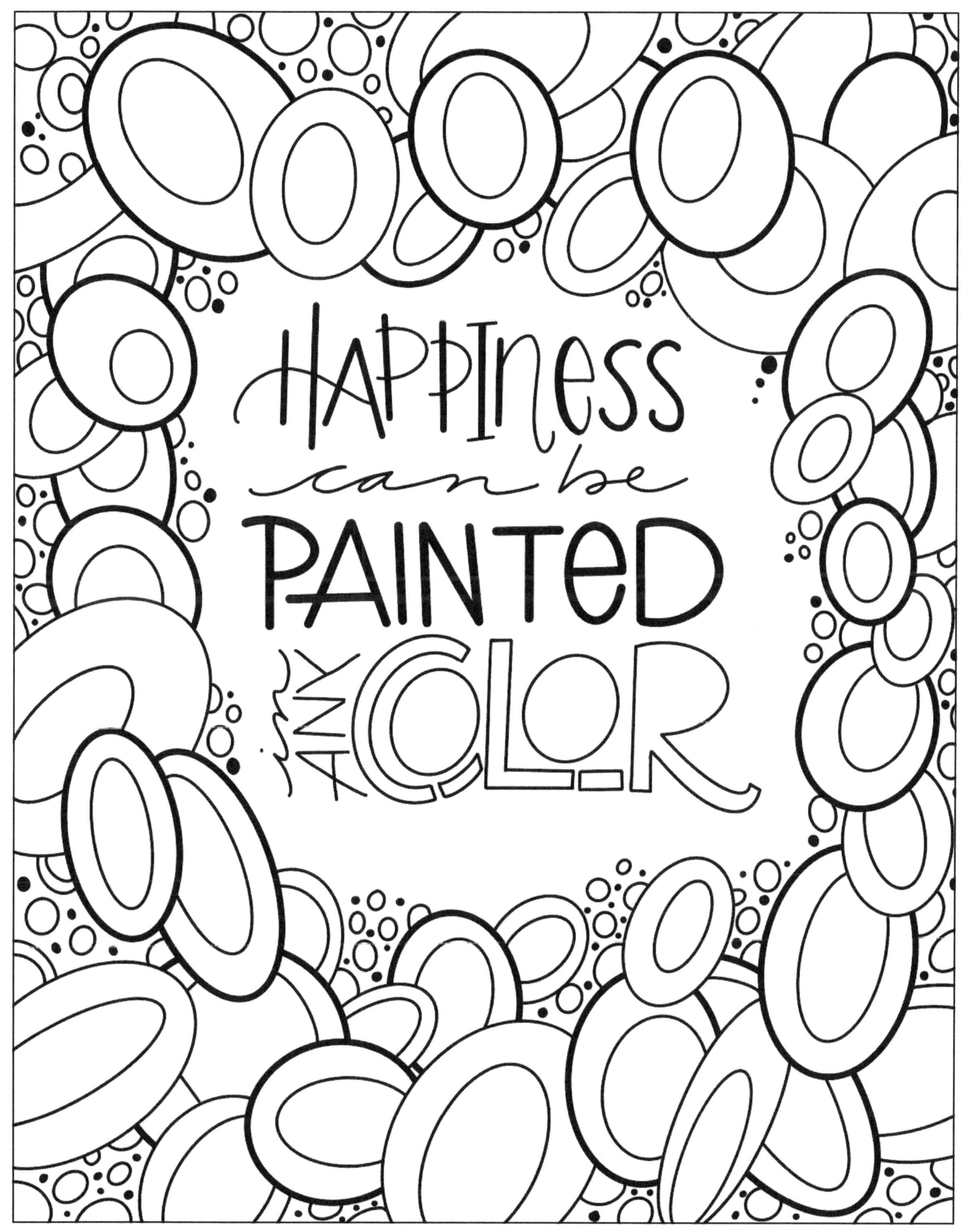

Happiness
can be
PAINTED
any COLOR

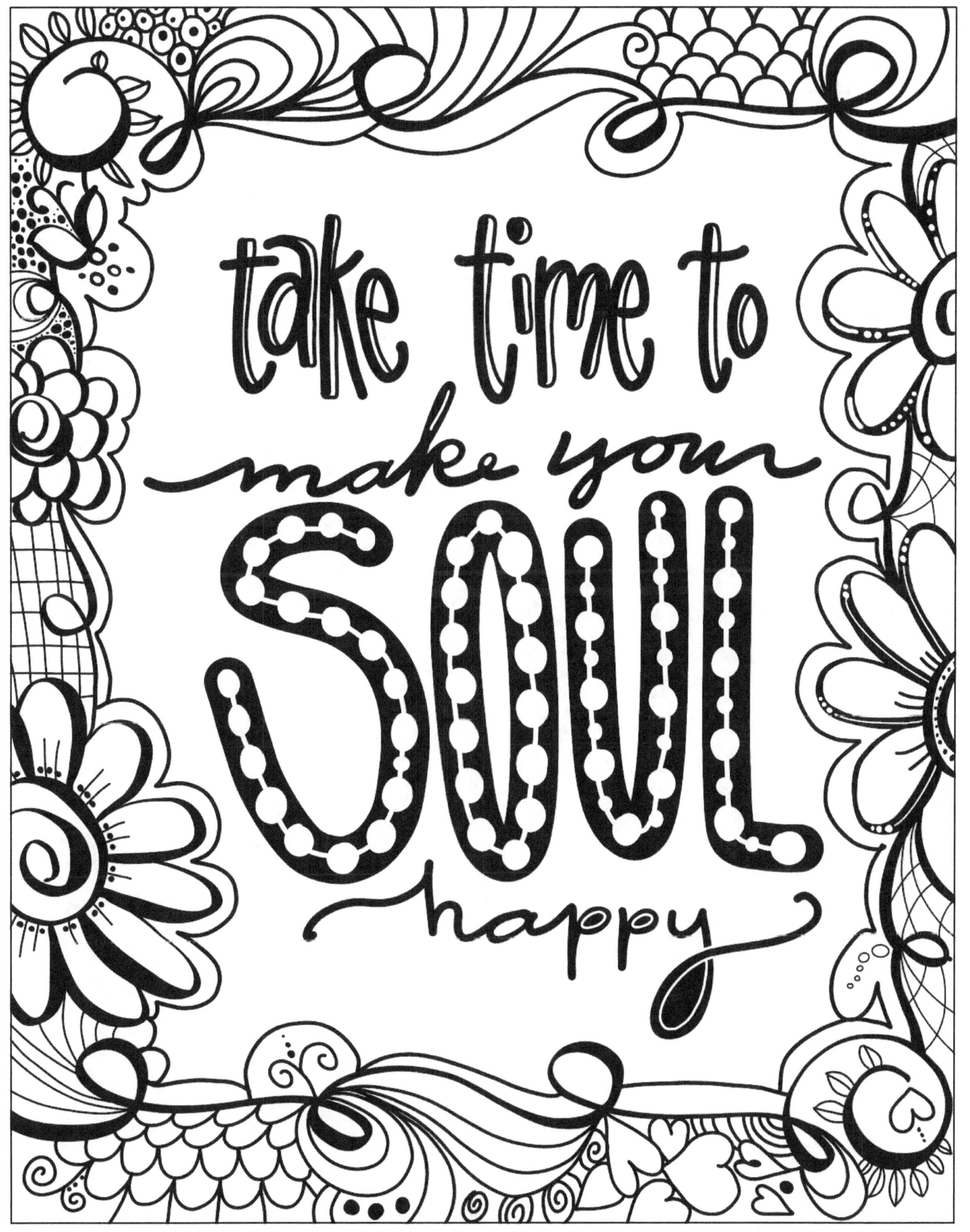

take time to
make your
SOUL
happy

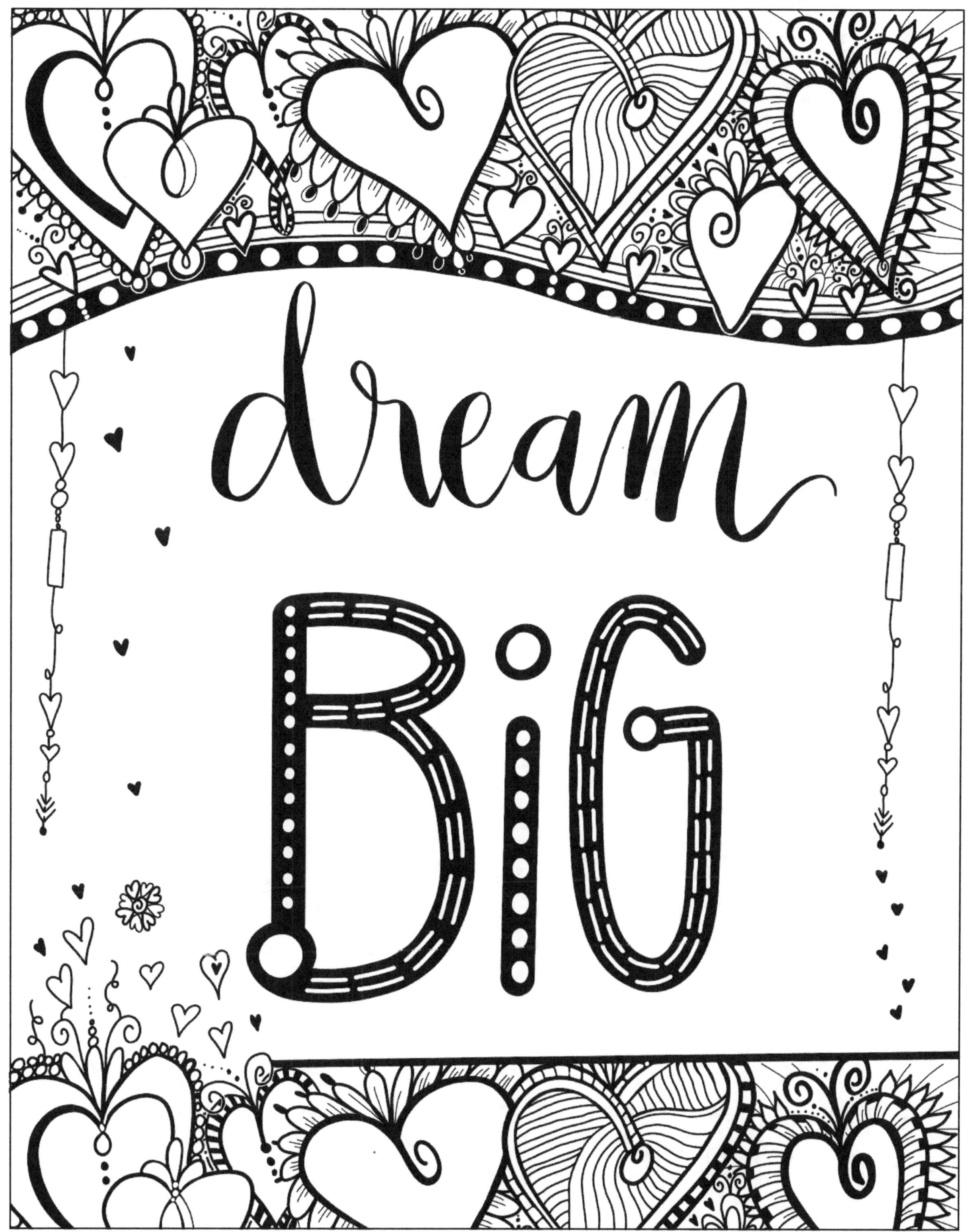

dream
BiG

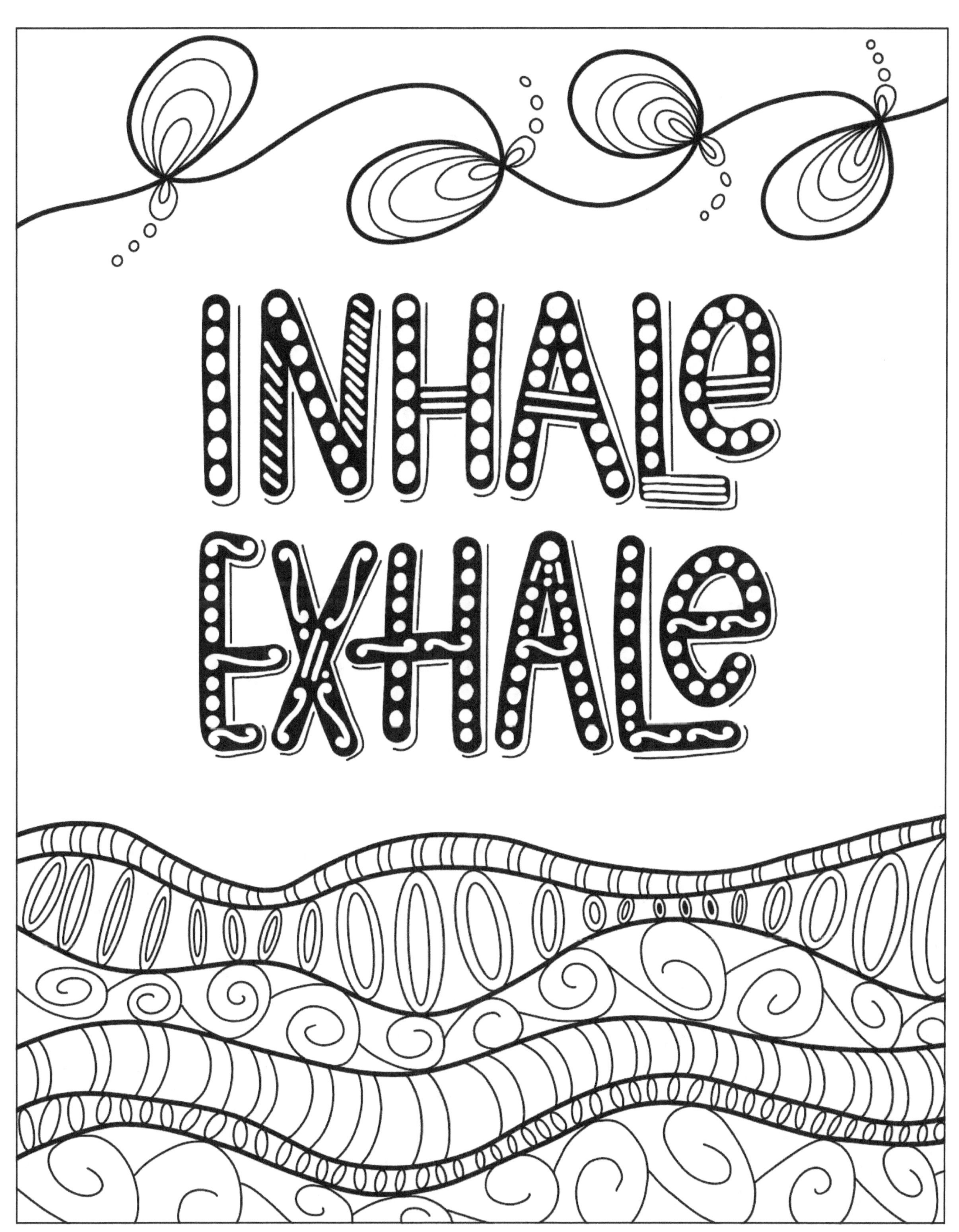
INHALE
EXHALE

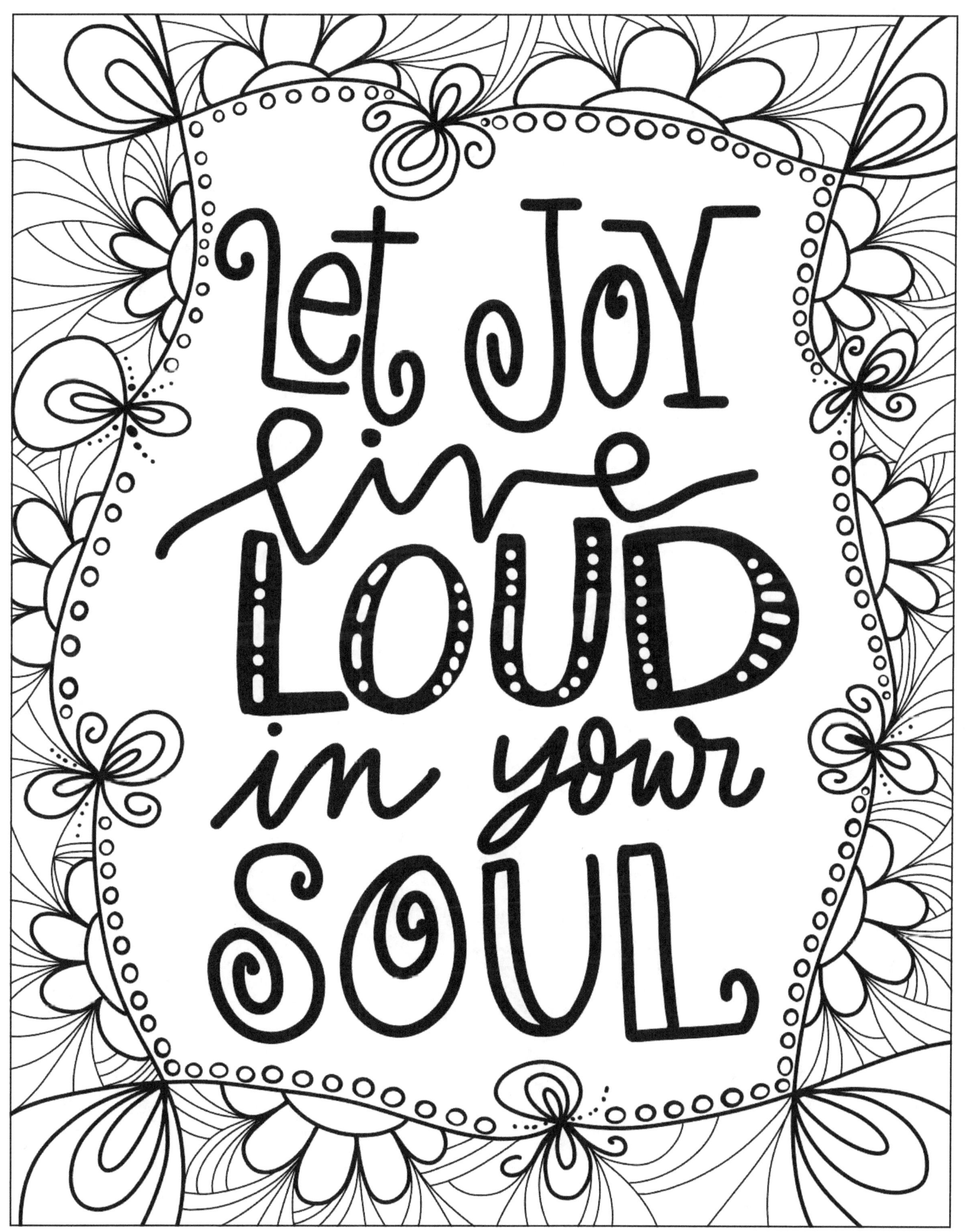

Let Joy live LOUD in your SOUL

## ABOUT THE AUTHOR

Roxanne Glaser is a versatile watercolor and hand lettering artist, certified yoga instructor, and self-proclaimed pen enthusiast who infuses joy into her art and illustrations. Her creative journey has been a source of solace and transformation, helping her process the profound grief of losing her husband and sister, as well as rebuilding her life after a devastating house fire.

Drawing inspiration from nature, her personal yoga practice, and copious amounts of coffee, Roxanne's artwork resonates with themes of transformation, encouragement, and gratitude. She shares her passion for creativity and gratitude through workshops, enabling others to reconnect with their authentic selves.

While the designs and patterns in this book are for personal use only, you can find Roxanne's work and creative courses online at www.superdoodlegirl.com.

Her coloring books and journals are also available for purchase on Amazon.

For bulk orders or to schedule Roxanne for a virtual or in-person visit with your group, please contact us directly at www.superdoodlegirl.com.